The ABC's of GOLF

by Dan Kirby

1st EDITION

Coyote Publishers

The ABC's of Golf. Copyright @ 1997 by Daniel L. Kirby.

Jacket design: Guy Goffredo of Studio Antocomp 282-2001

Published by Coyote Publishers, P.O. Box 1380, Kahnawake, Quebec, J0L 1B0.

Canadian Cataloguing in Publication Data
Kirby, Dan, 1941-
The ABC's of Golf
Includes index.
ISBN 0-9680813-0-4
1.Golf. I. Title.
GV965.K57 1996 796.352'3   C96-900390-0

1. Self Publishing - Canada   1st Edition

ATTENTION PROFESSIONAL
ORGANIZATIONS;
Quantity discounts are available
on bulk purchases of this book for
educational training purposes,
fund-raising or gift giving.
For information contact
Coyote Publishers,
P.O. Box 1380, Kahnawake,
Quebec J0L 1B0

Coyote Publishers

Golf, like a juggler on a unicycle, requires balance, co-ordination and practice.

Which do you think is easier to learn?

LIST OF ILLUSTRATIONS

TABLE OF CONTENTS

ACKNOWLEDGEMENTS

My wife and assistant, Arlene, deserves special thanks for working so laboriously to unscramble all the mumbo jumbo and make it understandable.

I want to thank Joyce Holmes for reviewing the material and suggesting the needed corrections and to Carly Goodleaf for her contributions and patience.

Many thanks to John Bartley whose suggestions are greatly appreciated.

Thanks also go to my son, Kariwate (Daniel), Wayne Zachary and Roger (Owhista) Deschamps who served so willingly as my models.

This book would not be possible if it were not for my silent teachers by their example, style of play and attitude, I became their 'golf child'. Thanks guys – Herbie Kirby, Frank Delisle, George Hemlock, Lester Zachary and the late George (the Mule) Cross.

I dedicate this book to ALL my fellow golfers, beginners and experienced alike.

ABOUT THE AUTHOR

Dan Kirby is a North American native from the Kahnawake Mohawk reserve. But his early years were spent in the south end of Boston. Since 1959, Dan has combined the skills of a high steel worker and a tree surgeon working at both sometimes concurrently.

Never one to be inactive, he is also an inventor holding two patents and is currently working on his third. He is also proud of the invention of a word game called "No Ifs or Buts".

He attended the Golfsmith School of Austin, Texas,obtaining his certificate as a clubmaker. Dan is also a certified golf teacher and operates a golf school.

For the past twenty five years, Dan has consistently been playing competitive golf. He has participated in the Canadian Quebec and the Mid Amateur tournaments as well as the Quebec and Jamaica Opens. He has also participated in the qualifying rounds of the U.S. Amateur and the U.S. Open Seniors.

Dan's latest achievement includes not only writing and completing the ABC's of Golf in two and a half months but doing all his own artwork as well and then transposing the illustrations to accomodate the left handed golfer. In addition to joining the ranks of other native authors, he is also a self-publisher. His satisfaction comes from the completion of his objectives. Learning to him is like space - there is no end and that brings us to his philosohy: **No one person knows it all and no one person ever will.**

He wrote this book because he believes that you can play a better game of golf by not only knowing the basics but also to relate your knowledge and experience to the golf swing and the golf game.

To contact the author:
For any instructional information or services about golf, direct your letters to the address below. Feel free to contact the author with comments and/or ideas for future editions.

Dan Kirby: P.O. Box 773, Kahnawake, Quebec, J0L 1B0

INTRODUCTION

Are you 100% satisfied with your golf game? Do you feel that there is room for improvement? Which of the two do you most often experience when you play golf - fun or frustration? Do you play golf your way?

I ask these questions because my experience and observation has convinced me that there are three major areas that people need to acquaint themselves with when it comes to golf.

A.   All golfers need to know the basics or the ABC's of golf. It is the substratum to all future learning about this game.

B.   The golf swing is part of your personality. It is your identity. Your abilities and talents are expressed in your golf swing. Copies or clones have no identity.

C.   Learn to learn in fun. People experience more frustration than fun in this game. Why? People lose sight of the fact that golf is a recreational activity and is meant to be fun and enjoyable. Fun does not breed frustration, anxiety and anger, competition does.

Golf is considered to be a fun sport, yet, watching some golfers, you wouldn't think so.

Learning to play golf should be as easy as learning the ABC's. I believe that if you do not learn to play the golf game in fun, it will not be fun to play.

An older man was once asked if he would like to know everything there is to know about life. "No", was his reply. Why? "Because there is too much fun in learning", he laughingly replied.

There is no question that combining a good teacher with the right atmosphere will make learning more educational and fun. However, most of us are not that fortunate. We just have to make do with what is available.

To make learning golf easy and fun for you, I want you to draw upon your knowledge and your experiences in life and relate them to the golf swing and the golf game. Relate golf through your eyes of understanding. Learning, at first, is like a morning haze. Nothing is clear at first but as the haze dissipates, figures begin to form and a sense of joy and relief come over you. When the haze disappears and everything is visible to you, you are happy and thankful. It's like watching a polaroid picture coming into focus.

At first, learning the ABC's of golf is not going to be clear but as you learn and see how the **posture**, the **grip**, the **alignment** and **ball position** all play a major role in the set-up, the learning process becomes fun.

We have all seen or heard of someone who reminds us of a family member, friend or colleague. In like manner, when we see something that reminds us of a particular golf maneuver, that association will help us to remember it in the future. There are oodles of examples that we can relate the golf swing to. For instance, a bowler who takes the ball back and rolls it to the intended target and follows through, resulting in a high finish. So, how does a housewife, a mechanic, a businessman or a gardener relate to golf? "There is always something there to remind me" is a line from a well-known song and it is so apropos. Past experiences coupled with **creative** imagination will aid your memory.

My job as an ironworker requires balance when swinging a 12-lb sledge hammer in mid air. Balance is required for walking narrow beams. We learn how to improvise when fitting steel to steel. As a tree surgeon, taking down trees differed from property to property. A golf swing **differs** from person to person. When you relate your personal experiences and save them throughout your learning, you're burning an impression on your mind and like a branding iron, it leaves its trademark.

If you find that learning golf is a little difficult, think of something in your lifetime that was difficult to learn and relate it to your present situation. Your problem becomes solvable.

When you learn in fun, you avoid "beating yourself" as the game does to many golfers. Golf doesn't beat you, you beat yourself. When you learn in fun, your approach to the game will make a world of difference. Remember, if you do not learn to play this game in fun, it will not be fun to play. Learning in fun should be tension free. No pressure. This will carry over into your golf game. **Golf is a recreational game.**

I encourage you to take and record notes, preserve clippings and/or pictures, anything that will serve as useful aids.

I have taken special care to transpose the illustrations so that you left-handed players will be better able to understand and utilize the information.

My artwork, though not perfect, nevertheless serves as a starting point, a model from which to work. The book is not concerned with minute details because I feel that they are needless and frivolous. I want you to capture the **over-all** view because, eventually, you will develop your own swing style - one that will suit your own physical stature and abilities.

The suggestions given in the ABC's of Golf will help to minimize your golfing problems and save you strokes. If you think of other ways to accomplish the same goal, by all means, use it.

I'm a firm believer in the old axiom, "If it isn't broken, don't fix it". Whatever works for you, stay with it. As a golf teacher, I believe that a person expresses his individuality through his golf swing. Golfers who copy or imitate others deprive themselves of that individuality thereby becoming only clones of someone else. **Clones have no personal identity.**

Above all else we need to know the essentials, the basics or the ABC's of golf. By combining these three elements, we will ensure a better and satisfying golf game and we will always have something to fall back on for support.

Do yourself a favor. Learn to learn in fun with the ABC's of Golf.

CHAPTER

THE IRRESISTIBLE FORCE

Did you know that there are more than 20 million Americans who play this sport annually? The projected number of Americans playing golf by the year 2000 will be 40 million. These numbers do not include people from Canada or the rest of the world.

Golf's magnetism is irresistible, so much so that even its former critics have been drawn in by its subtle and gripping power. Interestingly, golf can be described as having the 'power to produce an effect without using coercion.'

A game that was once upon a time played only by the privileged few has now become a game for all. It has become an internationally played sport. Golf's army of confederates include all age groups, male and female. People from all walks of life and vocations freely and eagerly participate in this game.

The increasing numbers have caused increasing demands. More and more golf courses have been developed throughout the country and the world. Golf equipment such as clubs, apparel, accessories and other paraphernalia, is in vast quantities at the retail store, golf stores and the local pro shop. The advertising and promoting of golf lessons and golf schools are practically becoming like your local neighborhood grocery store. Golf literature has skyrocketed. A 24-hour golf channel is in the living room of every zealot. Meeting the demands of golf has taken on gigantic proportions.

This 'irresistible force' is making its presence felt like an innocuous influenza!

You may well ask yourself, since there are so many books on golf, **why** another book on golf? What else could possibly be said about golf that hasn't been said already? Before I answer these questions and other related matters, let me share some tidbits about myself. To your surprise, you may learn that we have a few things in common. In fact, we do, GOLF!

CHAPTER **2**

MY EXPERIENCE

Maybe this title should read 'Golf's experience with me.'

My early years were spent growing up in the south end of Boston, Massachusetts, where baseball was everyone's passion. It wasn't until my family returned home to an Indian Reservation in Canada that my first contact with golf took place. There, it wasn't baseball that was every boy's pastime, it was lacrosse and hockey. Any youngster who wanted to make money would caddy at the Kanawaki golf club. I happened to be one of those youngsters.

Years later, back in the Boston area in the early '60's, golf once again came into my life through my father-in-law who needed not so much my company but transportation to the golf course. Reluctantly, I obliged. This company and transportation routine became habit forming and soon I was hooked. I have to confess, however, that is was at first more the 'nineteenth hole' than golf itself that caught my attention.

At the time, my brother, Herbie, was a member of the Ponkapong Golf Club in Canton, Massachusetts and through him, my father-in-law and I were able to play with a large group of new friends on the week-ends. As time passed, I became increasingly impressed with the more experienced golfers and their shot-making skills. However, it wasn't until the mid '60s, back home in Canada, that I had the privilege of playing with five experienced golfers who truly had a positive effect on me. Their shot-making was something to behold. Their chipping and putting were formidable and their driving and iron play were awesome. Each had his own style of swing and his own way of playing the game. Playing golf with them was like, as the expression goes, skinning a cat and through them I learned that there was more than **one** way to make a par. They deserve an honorable mention - Frank Delisle, Lester Zachary, George Cross, George Hemlock and Herbie Kirby. They were not pros but they were, in their heyday, the stars.

Among the five players, George (the Mule) Cross was the most unorthodox. George was about 5'7" tall, had very tanned skin and part of his left ear lobe was missing. He played cross-handed and putted with a 2-iron. He had a golf bag that was full of mixed clubs, both men's and women's. Even though he was a cross-handed player, he was a great ball striker. His low hook combined with his cross-handed grip gave him an extra sidespin and distance. I have yet to see another golfer hit a driver from the rough and get the distance that he did. George would rather run the ball on to the green instead of using a lob shot. I've seen him play through the trees, running the ball through the rough along the fairway, through the bunker and on to the green. You could never count George out of the hole. Once he was on the green, he would take out his 2-iron and easily sink a 30 foot putt.

The greatest lesson that I learned from these fellows was humility. At no time did any one of them brag that he was the best. Each and every one of us took turns at winning and if you happened to be hot that day and they were not, then it was your day. There was no 'lording it over' attitude from anyone. As for myself, playing alongside them, observing them and learning from them, made me all the better for their positive association. After more than twenty years of competitive golf, and still going, I can say in all honesty that I have never had more fun and excitement in playing this game than I have had playing alongside my mentors.

I would have truly loved to pursue golf as my chosen career but the combined responsibilities of family and a couple of occupations made that virtually impossible. My work as a tree surgeon and in high steel construction had also taken a toll on my back and I have come close, on several occasions, to giving up golf altogether. Fortunately, some sound advice and a fifteen minute routine of back exercises done faithfully every morning, has helped to keep me on the golf links.

I am one of those people who must always be busy and my spare time has given me the opportunity to come up with a safety invention for automobiles that break down on the highways. It's called the Kirby's auto "S.O.S." flag and comes in two versions, clip on and magnetic, and both are patented in Canada and the U.S. Another invention is a game called "No Ifs And/or Buts". It's a word game that requires selecting a subject to talk about and doing so without using the words most often used in the English language, **if, but, perhaps, maybe** and **appreciate**. The object of the game is to expand your vocabulary and develop listening skills. After I finished with that, I took a course on golf teaching, golf repair and clubmaking. This had added another dimension to my understanding of the golf game and golf equipment.

Making use of my spare time has now allowed me to become a writer and what makes a better subject for a golfer than GOLF? Actually, this project began as my personal reference work to be used as a teaching aid in my golf school. I liked it so much I thought others would enjoy and benefit from it as well. So, now, here I am sharing it with you in the form of this book.

The material in this book is not **dogmatic.** It's not a 'must do or don't do' set of instructions. The book provides guidelines, suggestions and helpful hints that you can adopt or discard at your discretion. If any material applies to you, fine. If not, discard it. People who have a set swing and a set mind can read it at their leisure. I do ask, however, that you contribute your thoughts and incorporate your ideas when reading over the material and doing the drills that you find most useful to you. **Allow** your imagination to run with you and look for ideas that would be helpful to you. Ask yourself how you can take this material and make it work for you. Make it your own.

Eighty percent of the golf swing is summed up in two words. SET UP. Pictures are provided as visual aids. Not only will you get to see how the pros set up but also how different they are. Consider this book as an aid manual and me as your guidance teacher. This book will also assist those who, otherwise, cannot get golf lessons or those who need golf lessons. Beginners in particular need more assistance in understanding the game of golf and how it should be played. It is still applicable to everyone.

My experience with golf and golf's experience with me has given me this opportunity to share some helpful thoughts. I believe that learning golf should be as easy as learning the ABC's. The XYZ's will follow. Once you learn the basics, the rest will follow.

CHAPTER **3**

THE YELLOW PAGES OF GOLF

Stop by any good book store and you'll find oodles and oodles of literature on golf. Writers and advertising agencies have flooded the market with so much information that finding just what you need can be daunting. We have such a 'yellow pages' of golf that even television has a special 24-hour channel devoted exclusively to golf. You can watch golf tournaments, get golf tips, golf lessons, tips on golf travel, find out about the latest golf equipment and call in to a television show featuring famous guests and ask them questions about golf. If you are a golf nut, then this channel is heaven on earth for you. In fact, golf today is a **fifteen billion dollar** a year industry. The one drawback to this vast supply of knowledge is that not **all** information may apply to you.

As a beginner, all this information thrown your way can be very confusing." Where do I start? What do I buy? and How do I know what's best for me?" are just a few of the questions you will have. You may already play golf but you have a problem and can't seem to get the results you want. Your questions could range from "What am I doing wrong? to "Do I have the proper equipment?"

In golf, as in anything else, we have to start at the beginning, the ABC's so to speak. A child must learn how to crawl before he can learn how to walk and walk before he can run. So too in golf. To start, the only information that beginners need to focus on is learning the **basics.** The basics of golf is the substratum on which all following knowledge will rest. It is the basics you will review when your game isn't up to par. How many times have you heard the expression 'back to the basics' when a team or an individual is experiencing a losing streak or a dry spell?

Understanding is the key to learning and once you understand how and why the basics work, everything else will fall into place.

This book is an addition to the 'yellow pages' of golf and its aim is to teach you to play golf your way and have some FUN while you're learning.

CHAPTER **4**

HAVE FUN - DO IT YOUR WAY

With so much advertising about golf equipment and merchandising, the industry would have you believe that buying a certain kind of golf hat, sunglasses or special clubs can give you longer drives and make you a better golfer. This is not only ludicrous, it's unrealistic! and buying into such salesmanship is tantamount to saying that buying a hammer and saw is going to make you a better carpenter.

Every golfer would like to lower his/her handicap and play a better and more enjoyable game. It's only natural. Have you ever peered into the mirror and seen yourself as Fred Couples or Nancy Lopez? We all wish we could play at the level of these champions and there is nothing wrong with wishing and hoping. There is also nothing wrong with having high expectations and wanting to achieve a higher degree of skill. But, back to the mirror. It should reflect the true you, you as you really are. Leave all the impersonations to the impersonators, to the Rich Littles and Jim Careys. The important thing is being yourself, working with what you have and making the best of it.

I would like you to see and play golf **your** way, develop **your** skills and really enjoy the game, and have fun at it. My objective is to have you pick and choose from the following pages the sections that are applicable to you.

Golf instruction manuals are nothing more than repeats and mine is no different except in its presentation. It's like a plate of pasta. Until you put something on it, it's only a plate of pasta. What do you like on yours? Believe it or not, some just like plain pasta, some like it with a simple marinara sauce. Others like meat sauce, meatballs and still others prefer garlic or seafood with their pasta. The point of all this is that it is **your** choice. It's what you enjoy.

Just as we don't **all** eat pasta in the same way, we **all** don't dress alike, we **all** don't drive the same kind of car, we **all** don't live in the same model homes and neither do we **all** have the same wives.

CHAPTER **5**

BE REALISTIC

The dictionary defines the word realistic as "seeing things as they really are" and a realist as "a person interested in fact and practicality rather than what is imaginary or theoretical."

Have you ever thought of running in the Boston Marathon? How about driving in the Indy 500 or competing in the Olympics? Do you want to be a world class golfer? All attainable goals to be sure, attained by those special and gifted people who readily and willingly suffer and sacrifice for their goals. You may be one of those people and that's great; but for the rest of us ordinary Joes, we're content to just sit back and watch, admire and maybe do a little wishful thinking. Why? because we're realistic that's why. We can run but can we run 26 miles? We drive but not at 200 mph. We do sports but hardly at the Olympic level and, of course, we play golf as best we can.

We are not being pessimistic when we say we can't do that. We are just being realistic. As much as we'd like to be at their competitive level, we're honest enough to admit that we're not in their league. It's a matter of knowing not only your strengths and capabilities but your weaknesses as well. Youth has inexperience and impatience to cope with and age can sometimes be blind to reduced agility, fooling themselves into thinking that they still have the vim and vigor of youth. The spirit is more than willing but the flesh is weak and this can lead to disappointment and loss of enjoyment. Avoid falling into this trap.

There is a vast chasm between a competitive golfer and the week-end golfer and still more with the casual, once-in-a-while player. The question you need to ask yourself is to what level and to what heights do you want to aspire and do you have what it takes to get there.

I, too, have had to stand in front of that mirror and ask myself those tough questions. Through most of my golfing years, I played amongst Canada's top amateurs but for the last couple of years, I have aspired to one specific senior event – the U.S. Senior Open at which I came in, at one time, as an alternate. I have taken into account my weaknesses and strengths. I know what it takes to succeed. But, I have to be realistic as financially I am limited to a few events. Nevertheless, I'm content to keep trying.

When you step up to your mirror, be honest with yourself, take stock, get to know your limits, if you have any, then **go** for it. You may very well have what it takes to be that world class golfer or you may be content with a round of golf now and then. Whatever your capabilities and/or limitations are, set realistic goals. Shakespeare once said, **"To thine own self be true"**. So must you.

CHAPTER **6**

HEALTH, AGE AND EXERCISE

A wise man once made an observation about youth and older people when he said, "The beauty of young men is their power and the splendor of old men is their grey-headedness." I guess he was talking about the strength, vitality and youth verses the brains of experienced elders.

The legends of golf and the senior tour players are great examples of age and health not preventing anyone from playing golf. In fact, I know of a nice little nine-hole golf course located near Lachute, Quebec, that caters to middle aged and senior golfers. Since electric carts are not allowed, the majority of the members carry their own bags. From the first tee, the landscape has a decidedly gradual incline and, believe me, if you are not in shape, you'll be really a-huffin and a-puffin. It's comforting to know that once you've reached the fifth tee, it's downhill all the way. Now if that isn't a perfect example of health, age and exercise all in one basket, then, I don't know what is.

When it comes to good health, no one age group has a monopoly. Everyone is subject to sickness and disease. Age, like a clock, keeps ticking ever forward. There is no turning back and no control. Those of us who are older can only reminisce about the days when, once upon a time, we were young. Today, we feel the aches and pains of the past sneaking up on us. Age takes its toll on our well-being so there is a need for us to be conscious of our health and our physical fitness.

Health is more controllable than age in that we control what we take into our bodies. They say you are what you eat. Junk food versus healthy foods.

Our bodies require fiber, vitamins and nutrients. Drinking lots of liquids and staying away from drinks with a high sugar content will help build our bodies instead of breaking down our system. Proper diet and exercise is a sure way to a healthier life.

Exercise is an important key to good health. Exercise does not kill people, **poor health does.** Exercise builds and strengthens the body and as we reach our middle and senior years, we need to be more conscious of our health and exercise accordingly. We should always remember to exercise within our limits, choosing from light to heavy duty work-outs, depending on our needs. Heavy duty work-outs and/or overdoing are not recommended for anyone not in good health. Twenty minutes a day of light exercise and stretching will keep us **supple** and in top shape. Have you ever noticed how a cat stretches after a nap? It's great for working out the kinks.

As we age, we need to be realistic as to what we can and cannot do, remembering that we're not as supple and agile as we once were. Playing golf requires body movement. Therefore, strengthening our legs, shoulders, hands and back will make our game more enjoyable and pain free. So make a light exercise schedule for yourself and stick to it. George Burns, the late centenarian, gave this bit of advice to his friend when he said, "Get out of bed and do things." There are oodles of fifty, sixty and seventy year olds who play golf and still play a decent game. They may look fifty plus but they feel thirty and sometimes act like eighteen. So, get out there, do something, if golf so happens to be one of your activities, go for it.

Seniors who play occasionally have no need to carry a heavy bagful of clubs. In 1913, Francis Ouimet, an amateur, won the U.S. Open with only seven clubs in his bag. Today, it's easy to find lofted clubs that can be substituted for your irons. Why carry excess luggage?

If you find that your clubs are feeling heavy, see a local clubmaker and check out your swing speed and swing weight. Try playing with lighter swing weight clubs or lighter weight shafts. I've seen all too often, women golfers using heavy swing weight clubs with little success. As with them, too heavy a swing weight will and does affect your golf swing. Swinging a club shouldn't be a chore. Instead, your club and swing should feel featherlike. Believe me, you'll enjoy your game much better. While you are at your clubmaker, have him check out your grips to see if they are adequate for your hand size. If not, change them. Never overlook a worn or loose grip, as little things overlooked can cause you big problems.

CHAPTER

IS GOLF REALLY FUN?

Let me imitate Andy Rooney of 60 Minutes to answer this question.

Is golf really fun? I'm trying for the life of me to understand how you can associate golf with fun. Fun to me is playing with my grandchildren, going to a circus, amusement park, skiing, swimming or going on a picnic. Fun to me is laughter, cheerfulness, enjoyment and pleasure. Did the meaning of fun change somewhere during my life without my knowing about it? How can anyone have fun and be frustrated at the same time?

How can this game be called fun when golfers swear, break and throw their clubs, argue, have temper tantrums, talk and mutter to themselves? Yet, they swear they are having fun. They have fun beating their friends but do their friends have fun in losing? Is having fits of anger, frustration and throwing clubs fun? Is losing fun? Do wives answer the phone and say to the caller asking for you, "Oh, Dan is out having fun today?" How is it that wives do not associate golf with fun? The only fun part of this game that I see is that people must have a good time being frustrated. Maybe I should try playing golf. Now, wouldn't that be funny?

Yes, Andy, golf is fun. It's just that some of these golfers don't know how to have fun. When the game is taken too seriously, or when heavy betting becomes top priority, fun goes out the window. When winning at all cost and any cost is a priority, the game is no longer a fun sport.

The pros have fun and are more at ease when playing pro-ams, charity and mixed tournaments. These events are tension and anxiety free. The atmosphere is conducive to fun, laughter and joke-telling. A fun game or friendly game to the pros is when there is no pot of gold at the end of the rainbow. All this changes though when it comes to tournament time. It's back to work as tournament play is the pro's livelihood, his bread and butter.

Since the greater portion of golfers are not tournament players and do not earn a living from it, they can derive a greater enjoyment of the game by not taking it that seriously.

Focus and keep in mind that golf is meant to be played in fun. Whenever you notice that you are not enjoying the game, not having fun, then it's time to take stock and ask yourself why is it that you are not having fun. Could it be that one of the above mentioned reasons apply?

Maybe you feel inadequate or you've lost some of your confidence. Or, maybe you're going through a spell of bad golf. **Think!** Now would be a good time to use your imagination and think of ways to put the fun back into your game. Some of us, in my hometown, occasionally play a round of golf with only one club using it as a putter as well.

Some clubs have an annual 'monkey' golf tournament. It's one club of your choice and a putter. Have you ever tried playing six hole matches with three other golfers? You play and switch partners every six holes. This is a real fun game as everyone gets to play as partners and there's plenty to talk about afterwards. There are oodles of ways to **infuse** fun back into the game. All you have to do is use your imagination.

Most golf matches cannot be played without some sort of wager even if it's only for a cup of coffee. Keeping these games under control prevents them from getting out of control. **Allow** others to voice their suggestions and experiment. All too often one or two individuals control what type of games should be played. This too takes the fun out of the game.

Keeping these games under control prevents them from getting out of control. Fun golf is only fun to those who make it fun! We want to maintain the 'spirit' of fun and pleasure. Then, and only then, will the game of golf reward us with good shots and satisfying scores. Golf has alot to offer when it comes to fun and entertainment. Maybe we'll even get to see Andy on the course after all.

CHAPTER **8**

GOLF IMITATES LIFE

Art imitates life or is life imitating art? It may be stretching it a bit when I say that golf imitates life but it's an observation made from a life on the golf links.

As in life, golf is not bogey free. We, sometimes, do score those nasty triple and double digit numbers, times when everything seems to go wrong, making us feel like we're playing under 'Murphy's Law'. (Murphy's Law? If anything can go wrong, it will go wrong) As in life, golf puts our temperaments to the test, stretching our patience to its ultimate limit. Those of you with little or no patience know exactly what I'm talking about.

As in life, we are called upon to make daily decisions regarding home, work, school, etc. In golf, decisions have to be made in the selection of the appropriate club and how to execute a given golf shot.

Some people take golf seriously, too seriously. Others are happy-go-lucky and, like a duck, let the water (problems) roll off their backs. There are happy winners and never any happy losers.

Blame. It's always easier to blame someone or something else for mishitting a shot. We all do it, you even see the pros on television doing it. (As though every shot they make is executed to perfection) Some of these ego maniacs want the whole world to stand still while they hit a golf shot. That would be like asking the birds to stop their chirping and the planes overhead to shut down their engines. We always blame others rather than ourselves for our mistakes. Interestingly, golf can certainly reveal a lot about us.

The game can become the thrill of victory on some days and the agony of defeat on most days. In golf, as in life, we experience highs and lows but it's the highs that keep us going back for more. Those highs, those good days are great morale boosters. These are like the wonderful surprises and good experiences of life, a raise in pay, the mortgage is paid off, your child has graduated from college and **finally** left home! Golf, at times, is like a celebration or a wedding, an anniversary or a birth. Those are the times when a golfer has hit an awesome shot, blasted in from the bunker, sunk a 50-foot putt or the ultimate experience of all, the hole-in-one. Bring out the noisemakers and the horns because it's Miller time!

People who are happy and enjoy doing whatever comes naturally have a balanced view of life. Like the juggler, they are able to engage in and have fun in many other activities without getting upset. So, too, in golf. We need to have a balanced view of our swing and how we react to that swing. Learning to balance our golf swing and game will make playing this sport more pleasurable

Life at times doesn't have to be like hitting all those 'red lights', we do have 'green light' days too!

Golf, as in life, gives us something to do and something to talk about, gives us good news and bad news, and surprisingly, holds up a mirror giving us a reflection of our true selves.

CHAPTER

WOMEN GOLFERS

Many years ago, I had suggested to a friend that if he wanted to learn how to swing a golf club, then he should take the time to watch the professional women golfers. There are some aggressive female ball strikers but, by in large, most of them have that **fluid**-like swing that is a pleasure to watch. Some of them start their swing so slowly that it gives the impression of slow motion. Believe me, take the time to observe their swing closely and you'll learn some valuable lessons and techniques.

Some men are slowly coming out of their dark age mentality when it comes to women playing golf. Unfortunately, some of these men still believe that a woman's place is in the kitchen and keeping them barefoot and pregnant, so to speak, will keep them off the golf links. A prominent CBS golf analyst, was dismissed from his job for apparently making some politically incorrect remarks about women golfers. Think for a moment, men, where would you and I be without women?

My suggestion to women golfers is to have your clubs checked for proper swingweight and swing speed by a qualified clubmaker. Some clubs are too long or too short for women golfers. Grips need special attention, worn grips, loose grips need changing.

When having grips installed, make sure they 'fit' your hands - not too small, nor too large. Anyone that tells you that it's really not that important lacks understanding and experience. Avoid such a character. That is why I strongly suggest consulting a schooled clubmaker. It does make a difference.

A golfer is a golfer whether it be male or female. The suggestions given within these pages are applicable to all. My advice? Proper swingweight clubs, loft and lie, grips and maintain a firm grip throughout your swing. Happy golfing.

CHAPTER **10**

JUNIOR GOLFERS

There is a nine year old who can track down and neutralize computer bugs and an eleven year old who conducts a symphony orchestra. Mind you, these children may be the exceptions rather than the rule. However, it brings home a very important point. Young children have that special capacity to absorb and retain information. They are also great mimics of what they see and hear. Two stand-out examples of the golfing world are Ben Crenshaw and Tiger Woods who both began to play at an early age.

A very young child will automatically follow Dad's example and if you are practising around the house, then he, too, will be inclined to pick up a golf club and copy your motions. But, if you want to introduce your child to golf then the age of five seems a good time to start. It's best that he **initiate** the request. Pushing or forcing children to engage in an activity that is not to his liking doesn't make for fun.

A child of five needs only one club to begin with, preferably a lofted one. The object being is to get the ball airborne. Most fathers, who are already golfers, usually have an extra club in the closet so the most natural thing to do is to cut it down to fit the child. Right? Common mistake because the club is too heavy for a proper swing. This was okay when I was a kid as we were lucky even to have even a stick with a rock tied on the end. For today's youngsters, try using a lighter clubhead, shaft and grip and make a comparison. There will be a difference in his performance. Today clubheads, shafts and grips are available to fit all children.

When it comes to actually buying clubs for children, parents need to keep in mind that age, height and weight have a direct bearing on their choice. One size shoe does not fit all. It could be the same size but a different width. Have you ever tried wearing a smaller size shoe or one that is too large? Then, you know what I'm talking about.

Playing golf with youngsters in the back yard should be fun so make up games that they want to participate in. Allowing children to play at their own speed (with undue pressure) makes playing golf comfortable and enjoyable for them. Give needed guidance only when required. Children need to come into their own and like you they need to develop their own personalities. Parents need to emphasize **play and fun,** not competition

The best lesson that a junior can learn is to play golf in its purest form. Playing the ball as it lies, counting all the strokes taken (even the missed ones) and sink every putt. **That is golf in its purest form!** Teaching golf etiquette and how the game should be played is of the utmost importance. In order for a junior to make quick progress, encourage him, and pat him on the back. The best way to discourage your child is to criticize him and **it takes no brains, no talent and no character to criticize.** Progress comes in stages so parents need to be patient and supportive. Your child's input will become evident in due time.

Like adults ,juniors need to learn how to take their golfing mistakes in stride and not get upset when they make an errant shot. Juniors, too, have to know that not every shot is going to be on target and learn to make the most out of every given situation.

Juniors should look up to professionals who set a good example, not to those who get upset and slam their clubs, displaying poor sportsmanship. They need to learn that "ugly conduct" degrades the game of golf and themselves. All golfers, young and old, should remember that golf is considered a gentlemen's game and behave accordingly.

The late Julius Boros displayed a fine example of gentlemanly conduct and even temperament by taking the ups and downs of golf in his stride. His causal manner and calm appearance made golf look like a walk in the park. His **respect** for the game is what juniors need to cultivate in themselves. Learning respect at an early age and developing a mild temperament or, at least, self control, will have a profound effect on a junior's future, be it in golf or in his personal life.

It is vital to consider the golf club that your family will join. Make sure it is one that encourages juniors to play whether in a family unit or with others. I contend that more clubs should have and support more junior programs because, after all, the juniors of today could be tomorrow's champions.

CHAPTER **11**

GOLF LESSONS AND TEACHERS

"Don't ever take a golf lesson" was the advice given to Laura Davies of the LPGA from a friend and club pro in England.

Golf lessons are usually associated with beginners but that is not necessarily always the case. All of us, at one time or another, need a spot check to make sure everything is AOK. Oftentimes, advanced students need only a minor adjustment or just a pat on the back to secure their confidence.

Every golfer should know the basics of golf - the ABC's and the mechanics of the golf swing. Knowing the ABC's of golf is the substratum on which the rest of your learning will be built. Your XYZ's will have a firm foundation. Systematic lessons enable the student to learn in a step-by-step fashion and he can always use this instruction as a guide to chart his progress.

The object of golf lessons is for students to learn and put into practice what they learn. All students need to understand that there is no 'snap of the finger' or 'instant learning' to golf. Those who possess this attitude will experience only disappointment and frustration. More importantly, this type of attitude will prevent you from learning the game in fun.

Lessons help students to correct themselves as they develop their swing through application, patience and repetition. Just as everything takes time to grow, so, too, your golf growth. How quickly you learn will depend upon your personal input. Impatience impedes progress. No matter how good the golf instructor or how good the instructions are, it's all useless if the student does not **apply** himself.

Golf lessons should be easily explained and easily understood. Feel free to ask questions. If you can find an experienced golfer, a qualified teacher and clubmaker all rolled into one, you've hit the jackpot! Take advantage of all that he can offer you, draw upon his knowledge.

Do you have an intense desire to learn and to learn properly? Will you apply yourself? Only you can answer these questions.

TEACHERS

Let me begin by saying that it's too bad someone hasn't filed a malpractice suit against bad golf teachers. Bad golf teachers have been known to kill, deform and cripple a good golf swing. Bad golf teachers only **reinforce** bad teaching and bad swings. They have no systematic method or substance to their teaching, often times reading golf literature to be one step ahead of their students. Their concept is a ONE SWING FITS ALL solution.

This is like a doctor who prescribes the same medication to all his patients, regardless of their differing illnesses. Without a proper diagnosis, some doctors have even prescribed penicillin to patients who are allergic to penicillin.

Teaching golf is not as easy as it appears. For instance, how can you teach a man with **one arm** to swing a golf club like a man with two arms? You just can't. A person's physical make-up must be taken into consideration. Too many pseudo golf teachers **presume** to know about golf and do more damage than good. They ramble on like babbling idiots about their knowledge of golf. Keep this thought in mind, a preacher **proclaims**, a teacher **explains.**

Some people fool themselves into thinking that a low handicap golfer must be a good teacher because he plays the game so well. Nothing could be further from the truth. SELF TAUGHT GOLFERS teach exactly that, SELF TAUGHT WAYS. They perceive the golf swing and how the game should be played through their perception, not yours, trying to make you a clone. Clones have no personal identities.

As a potential student, BEWARE! Ask for credentials. Ask what golf academy he attended. Where? and When? How many years experience in golf, in teaching? Give him the third degree; it's your time and your money. Take nothing for granted! Any teacher worth his salt will appreciate your interest.

A qualified teacher who has your interest at heart will teach you what you need to know. An experienced teacher will instruct you in a systematic fashion beginning with the ABC's, making sure that you reap the benefits of his knowledge and experience. A concerned teacher will take into account your strengths and weaknesses. He will note any physical handicaps that may hamper your golf growth and teach you accordingly. A good teacher will give you results.

Is it necessary for the teacher to have experience? Most definitely, yes! Anyone can learn from a book but you can't get the 'hands-on feel' from a book.

I'm going to drive home the point by using the medical profession to explain. A female obstetrician knows from seeing that women giving birth suffer greatly during labor and delivery. Unless she herself has experienced childbirth, she cannot know the full extent of the pain. She doesn't know how it 'feels'.

Experienced golf teachers know because they have gone through the school of hard knocks. An experienced golf teacher adds an extra dimension, a depth of understanding, to any golf lesson. Inexperienced pseudo golf teachers talk a good game but fail to perform.

My advice? For better golf, take lessons from a qualified, experienced teacher. Accept nothing less.

CHAPTER **12**

SELF IDENTITY

Many times you hear of phrases or song lyrics that are immediately associated with one particular person. Sammy Davis Jr. with "I want to be me, I want to be me". Popeye, the cartoon character, has his own famous line. "I am what I am, I'm Popeye, the sailor man". And a professional clown has his own registered trademark make-up.

Just like these characters, we all need to recognize our own self identities. All too often, in golf as in life, you hear phrases like "You can't do this" or "You can't do that". "Don't do this" or "Don't do that". Unfortunately, there is no end to such negativity and imposition. They tell you instead that you have to do it this way, their way, making you a carbon copy. Clones or carbon copies have no identities of their own.

Today, in Canada, some are teaching the swing styles of Moe Norman and the late George Knudson. The concepts and techniques are all well and good but these swing styles are unique to them. You may swing 'like' Moe Norman but you cannot 'think' like Moe Norman. By copying another style, you are, in essence, cramping and hindering the development of your own unique style. Just as there is only one Moe Norman, one Lee Trevino and one Jack Nicklaus remember, there is also only one of **you.** Think for yourself and you'll be happier for it.

In the past, a personal friend of mine (with a low handicap) had always refused to teach his friends the golf swing because the only style he knew was his own. He didn't feel right about teaching others his personal swing because he recognized that each person was different from him. Eventually, he went to a golf teaching school and now is able to teach others by helping them to make the most of their own swing styles.

Each and every person needs to express his own individuality. When we put a ceiling on ourselves or others, we impose on their preferences and we become limited. We deny and deprive our strengths and our development of character. Our abilities and talents should be unlimited. **Recognize** your talents, abilities and develop them.

When it comes to golf, the development of your golf swing is your identity. Your height, weight and physical make up will determine what type of swing you develop. Stay with what works for you; make the most of your own swing. Learning comes through trial and error and your innovative ways. Once you know the ABC's of golf, the rest is up to you.

DEVELOP AND MAINTAIN YOUR SELF IDENTITY

CHAPTER **13**

GOLF'S BUDDIES

Have you ever given any thought to how the weather affects your game and golf swing? Natural forces play such a very influential role in the outcome of every game. We probably never considered the sun, wind, rain and climate as a threat to our swing and eventual score, but think again. The weather affects us mentally, physically and emotionally. Have you ever noticed that your attitude differs with the change of weather? A beautiful sunny day brings smiles and cheerfulness. A dull, cloudy day has the opposite effect.

I like to imagine that the weather has it's own personalities and temperaments. For instance, there's Windy, Sunny, Rainy and Mr. Climate who can become humid, cold or sometimes behave like a perfect gentleman. Golf's buddies, good or bad, are your companions on the course and how you deal with them will determine your game plan and the outcome of your score.

Of all these characters, Wind is the most unpredictable and troublesome, even to the touring pros. The wind can make a par 3,150-yard hole into a 200-yard hole. By the same token, it can make it play like a 100-yard hole. It all depends on whether the wind is with us or against us. Note how the wind plays with our minds when it comes to selecting a club, and again, when we execute the swing. We become indecisive and indecision has caused many an errant golf shot. One minute, the wind is blowing in our favor; the next, it is directly against us. At other times, the wind can be blowing left to right, right to left, never quite making up it's mind on one set course. It's swirling motion keeps us second guessing ourselves. I swear, sometimes I think that the wind is having more fun than we are.

One of his best moves is his 'stop and go' routine. How many times have you experienced this situation? You have given considerable time and thought to selecting the proper club to play into the wind and just as you are about to strike the ball, the wind dies. How about the times when the wind picks up? Notice how it affects not only your mind but also your swing as well. Our golf shots end up too long or too short. As unpredictable as the wind is, we welcome him for his cool breezes on those hot, dog-days of summer.

PLAYING THE WIND

How can we play the wind? Texans are known to be good wind players. Everyone has his own method and if you have one that is successful, by all means, stay with it. Some have used the 'normal' set-up and the 'normal' swing, only using more club. Others use that low hit and run style. Then, we have the punch shot, a tricky little sucker that aborts your follow through.

Your punch shot begins with your normal swing, only use more club and grip down. Your follow through should stop about waist high, leaving your left arm pointing, as much as possible, at the intended target. Practising in the wind is fun because it is challenging and you have opportunities to invent different ways of manipulating your ball by your swing. The waist high drill will assist you in executing this shot.(Page 106) Take advantage of the practice center. Learn how the wind affects you and your swing. Once you understand how the wind carries your ball, you will be able to make the proper adjustments in any given situation. I repeat. **Use whatever works best for you.**

RAIN AND SUN

The rain and sun, however, are much more predictable. The rain is wet, slippery and uncomfortable. Keeping ourselves and, more importantly, our equipment dry is top priority. The hands need to be kept **dry** at all times in order to maintain control of the club. That is the reason you will see the touring pros carrying extra towels, extra gloves and rain gear in their golf bag. When we have a combination of old trouble-maker, Windy and his sometime friend, Rain, we know that we're in for a long day and high scores! Are you now beginning to see the influential role the weather has on your swing, game and eventual score?

And what of the sun? Sunny can either bathe us in his wonderful warmth or scorch us to toast. Bring on the humidity and we're now in for a steambath, very uncomfortable to some. The best advice here is to drink lots of liquids, water is best, and avoid getting sunstroke. If we're not in the best of health, common sense tells us that today is not a good day to play golf. Humidity creates sweaty hands. Sweaty hands make for a loose grip and a loose grip results in errant execution. So, keep your hands dry!

Climate varies throughout the world and we need to keep in mind just how these natural elements, golf's buddies, play a major role in our golf swing and game. Develop and learn to play accordingly and have fun doing it.

CHAPTER **14**

REPEAT OR PRACTISE - WHICH?

Simply put, golf is nothing more than repetition. Learning the 'set-up' and understanding the mechanics of the golf swing takes time and practice. Once you have developed a golf swing that feels comfortable and works best for you, maintain that swing. The rest is repetition.

ME? PRACTISE?

Since practicing is a matter of preference, some golfers choose not to practise for reasons known only to themselves. What gets me, though, is how upset these golfers get when they frequently hit errant shots! Any golfer who doesn't believe in practice should not expect miracles. Success depends on your personal input. You get back only what you put in or as the old saying goes, "You reap what you sow".

Specific practice makes for improvement - no practice makes for repeated mistakes. Mind you, there are a few golfers who possess natural abilities and talent that require very little or no practice at all. This, though, is a rare breed. Laura Davies of the L.P.G.A. is one of these.

Hitting golf balls for the sake of hitting golf balls is not practise, it's only a warm up or loosening-up exercise. Practising with a specific purpose in mind produces results. Golf improvement depends on personal input. Whether you are a beginner or not, there's no substitute for practice! How can **you** profit from practice?

WHY PRACTISE?

Just as people attend a fitness center to stay in shape, and sports competitors practise to remain in tip top condition, golf and golfers are no exception.

Practice in my day was not as promoted or encouraged as it is today. Practice was considered for beginners only since they needed to learn the game and gain some experience before playing. I, for one, never practised. It was strictly taboo. Do I regret it? No! I don't believe in that 'If I only knew then what I know now' nonsense. Each period of time is different and we live and base our decisions on what we know at the time. We can, however, learn from the past but we still have to make decisions on what we presently know. We have to be realistic and not dwell on the **ifs** in life.

Developing a self taught swing, along with determination, carried me through without practising until golf courses began to get crowded. Not being very patient, I wasn't about to spend 6 hours of stop and go golf. So, to kill time, I went to the practice center and began competing against myself. Target practice became a game to see how close I could get to the pin. Hitting irons, the 2-iron in particular, allowed me to take the club as far back as I could, and once I learned how to use it, it made all the other clubs easier to practice. Some teachers wouldn't recommend this today and I agree because the 2-iron is difficult to master. The 5-iron is the one recommended for practicing today.

Probably if more golfers viewed the driving range and practice field as a fitness center, maybe more golfers would go out and practise. Think of keeping your swing and game in tip top form by going out to the practice center. Practise **reinforces** learning!

I know a number of golfers who use their homes and backyards as a mini practice center. I've seen golfers hitting lob and approach shots around the house, over their houses, and chip at and into barrels. Some have even used their children's sandbox as a mini bunker. Putting in a room of one's house has become commonplace. This habit-forming practice is a sure way of developing a good short game, especially when **most** of our strokes are used up in this area of the game.

In order to get the maximum from your practice, if all possible, locate a practice center that has all the facilities to accommodate your game. These include bunkers, putting and chipping greens. The practice center affords us the opportunity to hit real balls which will help us to develop **feel.** When practising the swing, pay special attention to the feel you get when the ball leaves the clubface. I've seen many a golfer hit off-line drives and say afterwards, "Boy, that felt good".

Beginners shouldn't worry about ball flight direction at the outset of their lessons. This will follow as they progress. What I would like you to do is to capture that 'feeling' sensation, that gratification, that good feeling of getting your ball airborne and it will. This is where having a firm grip throughout your swing and making contact with the ball comes into play. Through practice only will you gradually notice or 'feel' when you are hitting the ball squarely, or if you're hitting it on the toe or the heel of the club. The sooner you acquire the feel, the quicker your golf improves. Just developing a feel is a good reason to keep practising.

Remember, once you develop a comfortable swing for yourself, groove it. Only practice and repetition will help maintain that groove. Consider ways to make your practice fruitful, be inventive. Practice builds confidence!

QUALITY PRACTICE

Be specific. Whenever you go to the practice center, have a goal, a specific purpose, in mind. What is it that you want to accomplish? Remember, hitting balls for the sake of hitting balls is not practice. We want to be mentally prepared and have a positive attitude. Visualize what you want to do, then, do it. Make your practice time **quality** time, time well spent. Here is a suggested list of things to do at the center and I want you to help by incorporating your own ideas into that list.

1.   Getting to know your clubs. Do you know what distance you can reach with each club? Is there any particular club that gives you difficulty? Do you spend time figuring out why? Is it your clubs or your swing that is creating the problem or both? Divorcing your clubs will not correct your swing. It could be that the lie on your club needs adjusting. So, the next outing to the practice center, note the yardage you can reach with each club.

2.   Bunkers - not bonkers. How well do you play out of fairway and greenside bunkers? Do bunkers intimidate you? A comforting thought to keep in mind as you learn to negotiate out of greenside bunkers is that they can be better friends to you than the tall and deep fescue surrounding the green. Whenever you practise out of bunkers, create for yourself **all** and **any lie** situations and blast away. Practise **open** clubface lies, and **closed** clubface lies for balls that are buried in the sand. Bunkers vary from green to green like pin placements. So, practice long, medium and short bunker shots, and as you do, take note of the type and texture of the sand without touching it. Is the sand wet, dry, soft or hard? Fairway bunkers differ from greenside bunkers and I'll touch on those in another heading.

3.   Target practice. Have you ever noticed that people who play darts, marksman, and archers have one thing in common? Target practice, targets to shoot at. Once you know what distance you can reach with each club, you can practise shooting at a specific target and see just how close you can come to hitting it. Make this a habit and you will notice a marked improvement. Since a lot of strokes are consumed by the short game, it would be advantageous to spend more time hitting targets from 150 yds. and working to the 50 and 25 yd. markers. Visualize and execute the shot.

4.   Compete against yourself. Using two golf balls, play a game against yourself. Play as though you are on a regular golf course and invent ways to improve your game, all the while repeating and developing **a feel** in your swing. Visualize what you want to do, then let it ride!

5.   Hitting into the wind. The game takes on a new dimension whenever we play against the wind – one of golf's buddies. It's nice to know the pros on the tour have to contend with nature's character and boy! can it cause problems. Side winds and winds directly in your face, winds left to right, right to left and swirling winds are a real challenge. As you practise against the wind, take your normal stance and use your normal swing, only use more club and grip down. Visualize, then do it.

Here are some valuable tips to keep in mind when practising and playing. When practising, **never** and I mean **never,** get down on yourself when you miss a shot. Stop and think what you did wrong and correct it. Crying over spilled milk is no solution. Take literal and mental notes. Learn to chart your progress. When playing with your friends, take note of how many fairways and greens you hit in regulation, how many putts you made and missed. What were the distances? Taking notes will indicate what areas need to be worked on. Often times, getting down on yourself only compounds a mistake. It's something even the pros experience.

Practise the low shots and the punch shots. When you practise, drop the balls to the ground and play them as they lie. Learning to hit the balls from different lie positions makes you a more knowledgeable and flexible golfer. Consider the wind conditions and practise accordingly. Trying to muscle a golf shot will, more often than not, work against you rather than for you. Again to reiterate, develop a swing that is successful and works best for you. Visualize your shot, then do it. Practice, practice, practice. It **reinforces** what you've learned.

Practice should result in your ability to execute your shots without even having to think about them. It should be second nature. To illustrate: When you awake in the morning, do you know which foot you put your sock on first, left or right? If you have to think about it, you don't know. What I'm getting at here is that by repeatedly practising the same shot, it will eventually come so naturally to you that you don't even have to think about it. It will become automatic.

Try these few suggestions, incorporate your own ideas, develop that special 'feel' only you will know and above all, develop a positive attitude toward practice. Make it enjoyable and worthwhile. You'll be rewarded with a sense of accomplishment. Go to the practice center with a **positive attitude** and leave with a **positive attitude!**

CHAPTER

THE MIND GAME

They say that golf is played between the ears. Golfers are known to talk themselves into missing putts and making errant shots. Narrow fairways give many golfers the jitters and they substitute irons over drivers. Golfers freeze up when they see a pond or a bunker in front of the green. Golfers play mind games against their fellow competitors by making suggestive remarks. What causes freezing and this power of suggestion to dominate us? What is it that triggers the mind to affect our emotions. Simply put, **thoughts!**

When any information is transmitted to the brain, we can allow it to affect us for the good or for the bad. Only by acting on this information do we accomplish the desired result. For instance, to complete a job or a project, you set your mind to it, but if you don't put your mind to it, the job drags on and is left unfinished. (you know what I mean)

The mind is such that we can dismiss what is unacceptable, choose what we like or, still yet, entertain other thoughts or even put it on a mental shelf to think over later. **Personal character** and **attitude** will determine the outcome of any given situation. Some minds can be easily influenced. Others are suspicious, doubtful or rock-solid. We can't turn off our minds just because we're out to have fun. The brain is forever active and we think about everything, even golf. The more moving parts you have in a machine (or an activity), the more chances of it breaking down.

Thoughts are transmitted to the brain area that will, in turn, relay signals to the appropriate receiving depot. Some messages will have a quick response. Others will be dismissed or put on hold till further notice. How many times have you waited for a friend to make up his mind? He's waiting for further information. "He that hesitates is lost" is another axiom that falls into the category of indecision. **Indecision** causes more errant shots than golfers playing peek-a-boo (heads up) golf.

When you're not sure what club to use in a given situation, or how much power to exert when hitting the ball, you have two thoughts and no definite plan. So, what happens? A miss hit execution because you couldn't make up your mind.

Do you get upset when you make an errant shot? What do you do? Do you show your feelings? Craig Statler is a sterling example of one who shows his emotions and reactions to his game. We all do it to some extent, some more so than others. When we make that error, do we let our feelings compound it by making another error? This happens every day. They call it 'losing your cool'.

The pros play a different level of golf, meaning that their concentration level is higher than ours. They cannot afford to be distracted as any **distraction** will unbalance their rhythm of thought. Some pros have a fixed or set mind. Others go into a trance-like state while we have still others who can zoom in and out at will. This latter group are the ones who can execute their shots and still carry on a conversation.

As a high steel worker and tree surgeon, I know firsthand how the mind works in relation to height and dangerous situations. This kind of job requires balance and co-ordination. I've been able to use this past experience in my golf strategy. It's not as though I have no fear of heights but I do have a very serious respect for heights and I wouldn't endanger myself or others by making thoughtless decisions. We all have fear of some sort, it's only natural. It's **how** we handle that fear or apprehension that's important. People have been known to scare themselves to a point where they can't function.

Only a few reach that level of fear while playing golf but it does go to show how our feelings can influence our game. We can actually beat ourselves by **feeding** our fears with negative thoughts, thereby, reinforcing our fears, time and time again. The weird thing is that we allow it to happen, we **allow** it to get the best of us.

I vividly remember when the R.C.G.A. held their first Mid-Amateur Tournament at Royal Montreal. After qualifying, I played my first two matches without so much as losing one hole to Don Brock from Kanawaki or to the player from Ottawa. Both matches ended on the fifteenth hole. As you can imagine, I was pumped and ready for bear! My next match was to be with Graham Cooke, the best amateur player of Quebec. While I was at the practice center before the match, something terrible happened. I accidentally broke my Taylor made three wood on a metal rack. It was my favorite club. I used this club as my driver and fairway wood. When it broke, **shock waves** went through my entire body. My favorite club was broken, I felt lost. I carried these disturbing thoughts and feelings throughout my match with Graham. It cost me the match. I lost on the very same hole on which I had beaten my previous two opponents. That's what the mind can do. Since then, I've had the shaft replaced three times but to no avail. This club is no longer with me. Broken clubs or stolen clubs are enough to get the mind off track and you pay the price for it. Steve Elkington had his clubs stolen from his vehicle, clubs that he'd had for years. I'm sure losing the clubs whose feel was so familiar to him must have been devastating. I lost just one club and I felt bad. Now, missing a short putt, or making a bad shot under pressure, is not the same as losing clubs but it still affects the mind.

We all miss short putts. However, the ones that trouble golfers are the ones they freeze over, having this strange phenomenon overtake them and be unable to do anything about it. Why only at certain times? **Fear!** Fear of crowds, fear of pressure, fear of winning or losing or maybe not believing in yourself. **Negative** thoughts produce **negative** results.

It's easy for me to sit back and make suggestions. Nevertheless, here are a few points that you may want to consider. When putting or hitting a golf shot, just go about your normal routine. If someone makes you nervous, putt out without stepping on their line. You're probably taking the game too seriously and putting undue pressure on yourself. The best advice I can give you is to **be yourself.** When playing golf, we have to be realistic because these strange and unusual swings and shots will and do occur. That's why they get on T.V. Bloopers.

We're not going to be in a positive mood every single minute so let's make the most of it. Turn a negative situation into a positive learning experience. If you're not going to be a touring pro, enjoy the game. All week, you anticipated this golf week-end, so enjoy it for what it is. A relaxing pastime.

MENTAL PREPAREDNESS

Which would you give more thought to - your ordinary chores or your vacation?

The answer is quite obvious. Ordinary chores do not require much planning. It's just a matter of going through a routine. On the other hand, planning a vacation, a wedding or moving to a new home requires a great deal of **forethought.**

In like manner, how you approach the game of golf will reflect your mental preparedness. Is your golf game just a routine - a going through the motions? Have you ever noticed how things perk up when we make plans for a vacation or a special event? Similarly, your golf game can come to life by **mapping** out a game plan. Take the time to think over your game plan. Leaving things to chance is like a dog chasing his own tail. **Allow** your imagination to flow freely and plan to accomplish at least one goal.

During any practice round of a tournament, I scout the landscape of the golf course and make mental notes. I take the time to ask the local club members a few pertinent questions. Where should I land the ball on the green in relation to the pin placement? Where are the hidden bunkers, hazards, and landing areas? Taking notes helps.

I find that the most important part of my golf game is my mental disposition. If I am not mentally prepared, my performance will not be up to par. *(No pun intended)*

These are just a few examples of what I do. It doesn't mean you have to do them as you may have areas of your own to work on. Maybe you need to work on getting unduly upset over a mis-hit shot. Repeatedly, I see golfers mis-hit a shot and make matters worse by letting it get the best of them. Consider it spilled milk and move on. Mental preparedness will ignore that mis-hit and if anything, is already planning for the next golf shot. Mental preparedness does not allow distractions to become a factor. Mental preparedness is like a train on a track - a one track mind. Organize a game plan and stick to it.

The only person controlling the destiny of your golf is YOU! To play better golf, set your mind to it.

CHAPTER  **16**

THE GOLF GREMLINS

This chapter is an extension of the mind game. I've named it the Golf Gremlins due to its devastating effect on golfers. I'm sure you've played with someone who talks himself into missing a short putt. Or, how about the golfer who cannot play a round of golf without three putting, double bogeying or who just can't seem to par a particular hole? These are but a few examples that may ring a bell.

The golf gremlins attack everyone but, more so, the inexperienced, the timid and the over-aggressive golfers. **We** create our own golf gremlins by convincing ourselves that we have limited abilities and talents. Negativity. At times, we can be our own worst enemies.

What can you do to combat these critters? Well, to begin with, you need to 'reinforce' your self confidence. You can do this by asking yourself a relevant question. What is it that prevents me from taking that forward step? Get to **know** your fears and work on overcoming them remembering always that if at first you don't succeed, try and try again. You need to **believe** in yourself.

It's comforting to know that some of the above-mentioned gremlins aren't really gremlins. How so? It could be as simple as misreading a putt or just so happen to hit a spike mark that knocks the ball off line or three putt from fifty to seventy feet. It happens to all of us.

There is a sign posted on one of the beaches in Cape Cod that reads "Accidents do not happen, they're caused". There are times when sheer thoughtlessness and carelessness on our part cause these costly mistakes.

To me the real gremlins are the 'yips' and the 'shanks', two gremlins that really play havoc with the mind. They come out of nowhere with no advance warning whatsoever. In short, the 'yips' are the putting shakes. The 'shank' is Mr. Gremlin, the master of masters because of his ability to embarrass and humiliate you. He doesn't know from left, right or center. This gremlin knows only a 90 degree departure from the clubhead.

How can you deal with these gremlins? Some have resorted to cross-handed putting to deal with the 'yips' while others take to using longer putters. Some have weathered the storm by simply letting the 'yips' take their natural course till they eventually peter out. There is one thing, however, that you want to definitely avoid and that is to keep entertaining the idea and allowing it to consume you. This is the time to think positive and do positive.

Many stories can be told about the infamous Mr. Shanks Gremlin, who he is and what he is. He has that unappealing trait of attacking you when you least expect it.

One of my shank stories happened to a fellow golf partner who was preparing to chip from the edge of the green to the pin fifteen feet directly in front of him. To his extreme right was a bunker and the only way the ball could possibly get into it was for him to shank. And that he did, straight into the bunker. I couldn't believe my eyes. Even more unbelievable was his story about the time he literally shanked around the green!

I, too, have had my run-in with this particular gremlin. It happened in Boston in the late seventies while I was trying to quality for the U.S. Amateur. I shanked eight balls in a row while practising. I had never shanked a ball before and it would be nice to say that I never shanked a shot again. But the important thing is that during my round of golf, I never once shanked a shot. Why? My mind was centered on qualifying. Nothing was allowed to distract me.

To deal with the shanks, you might want to try these two exercises. They're not really new ideas just not widely publicized. Place two balls side by side about two inches apart. Hit the one closest to you without touching the other. Repeat.

The other is, simply, to close the face of the club and make as though you're doing punch shots. **Sometimes, doing your own personal experimentation to counteract the problem will result in a solution.**

To reiterate, avoid letting your personal gremlins consume you. Know your fears and deal with them. **Consistently plant seeds of optimism.**

CHAPTER

CHIPPING AND PUTTING

Who isn't familiar with the motto "You drive for show and putt for dough"? Surprisingly, some golfers put more emphasis on driving than on putting. I wonder if playing a round of golf with the likes of Ben Crenshaw would change their minds.

Probably, like myself, you know someone who can chip and putt like a wizard. My brother, Herbie, is one of them. Whether he was on the fringe or on the green, you can be sure he was either in or very close to the hole. When asked the secret to his putting abilities, my brother would just say, "Either you have it or you don't". Some don't know, others guess and still others believe it's probably instinct. The latter would be correct.

Instinct is not a learned behavior. Many golfers learned or were taught how to putt and through time, practice and experience, developed a good putting habit. On the other hand, instinct is independent of experience. It's like common sense. There are no schools that teach common sense. It's an instinct. There are many people who are illiterate, yet, have common sense.

Instinctive putters are naturally gifted. They don't have to practice in order to become good putters. Bad putters need a few tips and proper guidance. Many golf magazines provide pictorials on putting drills and theory. Try them. If they work for you, use them.

Good putters visualize the ball going into the hole before even making a stroke. They size up the hole, looking for hidden breaks and note the distance they must cover to make the putt. Some putters pick a spot somewhere between themselves and the hole, then, roll the ball to that spot. Some pick a spot about a foot in front of themselves as a starting point. When a putt has a bend to it, go with the bend. When you drive a car and the road has a curve to it, what do you do? You go with the curve. Pick a spot where you think the ball will bend or break and **roll** it **to** that **spot.** Here's an old putting tip. When putts go from left to right or right to left, always favor the high side of the cup. Balls below the cup never drop in, balls above the cup do.

Many teachers recommend letting the ball die into the hole. I prefer to be a little longer. If you are going to be one foot short, six inches short or one inch short, why can't you be just as long? I've yet to see a short putt drop into the cup. Short putts or playing safe instills **timidness** and doesn't do any good for your confidence. **Confidence** is the key to good putting. Passing the cup by at least a foot gives a much better chance of the ball dropping into the hole than a short putt.

Squaring the putter to the hole and hitting the ball squarely on the putter blade, along with good body alignment, will improve your chances of sinking more putts, Beginners are taught to putt with the pendulum stroke motion. To illustrate that pendulum motion, get a large book or a shoe box and put it two inches behind the ball. Bring the putter back till it hits the box, then push the ball forward toward the intended target. You may and will double hit the ball but don't worry about it you're supposed to. You're working on developing a stroke. Try this same maneuver at various lengths up to six feet. It's great practice for those short putts.

Whenever you practice putting, practice all different lengths and situations. Learn to feel the ball coming off the putter head. Learn to roll the ball. Play games against yourself and never worry about missing putts or letting it get you down. Golf is only a pastime, a hobby. Avoid taking it too seriously.

Greens vary from one club to another. Common turfgrasses are bent grass and Bermuda for putting greens. It's good to keep this in mind because it most certainly affects your ball. Note whether the grain is with you or against you. **Speed, distance, feel and the direction of the grain** are the key things to remember.

Are you comfortable with your putter? If not, search out a schooled clubmaker as he can provide you with some valuable information. For instance, maybe your putter is too long or too short or you may want to change to a flat-top putter from a rounded grip or maybe your grip is worn and not tacky enough. Just as there are bad golf teachers, there will be bad clubmakers, so make sure of him. Ask around.

Bad putters never have to worry about the dreaded 'yips'. They just go about their merry way doing the best they can. Bernard Langer has had at least three separate experiences with the 'yips' but his determination to never give up and his stick-to-it attitude has paid off for him with tournament wins. What are the 'yips'? Who knows. A miscommunication between the brain and the hands? You know what you want to do but your hands don't obey. They push when they're supposed to pull, they snag when they're supposed to be smooth. Whatever they are and however they're described, they are definitely unnerving. It shatters confidence in one's ability to putt and leaves one uncertain and demoralized, forces you to try anything in a desperate attempt to rectify the problem.

If you are having trouble with the 'yips', try tucking your forearms to the side of your body and let your tummy help you push or stroke the ball to the hole until your confidence returns. If it doesn't work for you, you haven't lost anything. **Nothing ventured, nothing gained.**

Since putting is a matter of preference, do and stay with what works for you. Remember, there are more ways than one to achieve the same goal. You can go to New York city by plane, car, bus, motorcycle or a horse and buggy. You get the idea. However you execute your putt, keep in mind these few helpful hints, a **firm grip, proper body alignment,** a **squared putterhead** and hitting the ball on the **'sweet spot'**.

Golf etiquette: Avoid spiking greens. Tap down spike marks after putting. This shows consideration for your fellow golfers.

CHIPPING

The interesting thing about chipping is that you can use practically any club in your bag, almost anything goes. You have choices as to what kind of shot you want to execute. You can loft the ball in with a wedge. You can run the ball to the hole with a club as low as a 2-iron, even to using a wood. In fact, in the 1996 Quad City Classic, Tiger Woods used a wood from the fringe not once but twice and twice he was successful. Who then is to say what you should use? There are no laws that say you have to use a certain club for a particular shot. Some golfers, after having deliberately broken a putter, have finished the round using a driver to putt. It's true that the rules stipulate that you must have only fourteen clubs in your bag but there are no rules about having and using less.

The chipping stance or set-up varies from one golfer to another. A standard set-up is placing the feet closer together with an open stance and the ball being played off or near the right foot (big toe). You can place the ball anywhere you see fit as long as it **works** for you. The back swing is very short and you follow through as though you're putting. Your hand position is far back from the ball. This is a mini, mini version of the waist high to waist high drill. (See chapter 31)

LOB SHOTS

One of my golf buddies, nicknamed Roger "Buckwheat" Norton, has this shot down to a science. He plays this shot with a wedge, the same way he plays bunker shots with a reasonable lie. He opens the face of the club, makes like a slow motion swing causing the ball to be quickly airborne and lands it softly on the green and near the hole.

If one of your golfing companions is good at executing a particular shot, observe him, watch how he performs. Above all, freely **ask** him how he does it. He, too, had to learn it either through trial and error or by asking someone else. Ask! You have a lot to lose if you don't.

No one consistently hits the greens in regulation every time he or she plays a round of golf. In order to make pars, we have to scramble.This is where good scramblers are like street fighters - they know how to get out of clutch situations. Good scramblers are either good in making lob shots, chip shots and/or are good putters. As an example, in 1975 during my second round play of the Quebec open at Loretteville, Que., I hit 5 greens in regulation for a 75. My competitor hit 16 greens in regulation including an eagle for a 78 ! In short, the short game is what golf is all about. Pay attention to and practice your chipping and putting.

CHAPTER **18**

BUNKER PLAY

What to remember when playing from a fairway bunker vs. a greenside bunker.

Most fairway bunkers are straight away golf shots. The ball is usually sitting up which makes it that much easier to hit. When you are in the bunker, take your normal stance as you would in the fairway. Wiggle your feet into the sand so that you have a solid footing. Next, you want to grip down on the club about an inch or so. This is to give you better control of the club when you execute the shot. The object here is to hit the **ball first**, not the sand. Now, swing the club in your normal way and follow through. If you stopped for a coffee break, you're in trouble.

Question. Your ball is partially buried in the sand of a fairway bunker. What would you hit first, the ball or the sand? The object is to get the ball out of the bunker first. Never mind getting distance. We can see from this situation how the lie and distance are determining factors in executing a fairway bunker shot.

The greenside bunker set-up resembles a golfer who is going to slice with his driver. Our stance is open, making the left shoulder positioned left of the pin, and making the right shoulder face the pin. Again, we wiggle our feet into the sand. Next, we take the sand wedge and open the face almost to a flat position, then, grip it. Most golfers have a tendency to grip the club first, then open the face of the club causing a twisting of the hands. Try it and you'll see what I mean. There is no need to grip down on the club in this situation. Again, it comes down to using what works for you.

Now that you are set up to execute the shot, make sure that you hit the **sand** first, then follow through. No coffee break. How far away from the ball should you hit the sand? It varies with the placement of the pin. The closer you are to the pin, the more sand you need, even at times up to four inches behind the ball. Less sand is needed if you are farther away from the pin. Two or three inches should do.

A different set-up is called for when your ball is deeply buried. In order to get that ball out of the sand, you need to close the face of the club and **chop it out**. No follow through is required. Just get the ball out of the sand. Now is not the time to be concerned about getting close to the pin. Notice, also, that your stance differs from that of the blasting-out position. Take your normal stance and play the ball nearer to your right foot. The more you practise the bunker shots and experiment with the various **lies and distances**, the more confidence you will gain in executing the sand shots and assessing the amount of sand you need to take. Another thing you will learn by practising is to judge the sand conditions. Dry, wet, soft or hard, your knowledge of these differences will dictate how you play the shot. **Avoid** touching the sand when your ball is in the bunker because the bunker is a hazard.

Always keep in mind that bunkers are considered hazards and unintentional slips can inflate your score unnecessarily. For instance, grounding your club while your ball is in the bunker will cost you a two stroke penalty. Touching the sand on your **backswing**, even accidentally, is an infraction.

Here's another example. You stroked your ball in the bunker but it didn't come out. Out of disgust, you whacked the sand. This is an infraction which will cost you an automatic two stroke penalty. It is good to keep in mind that these situations and penalties apply to **all** hazards. Therefore, keeping mentally alert and staying cool will save you some crucial strokes.

One more suggestion. No golfer likes to play out of a shoe print so be considerate. Rake the sand after each time you use it and in so doing, you will be practicing golf etiquette. Remember, stay with the swing that **works** best for you. Practice your sand shots with both opened and closed clubface. Happy blasting!

BUNKER ILLUSTRATION

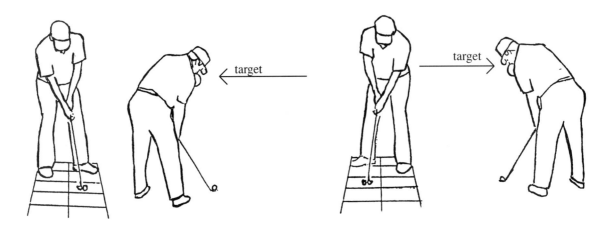

CHAPTER

WHAT THE PROS HAVE IN COMMON

No matter who we are, we all have some things in common. We all work, we all have hobbies or special interests, we all love recreation time and we all enjoy vacations. As golfers, we have the love of golf in common. However, it is the more specific traits that the pros have in common that I would like to share and through them, we can learn what makes them successful. It's true that we, as well as the pros, all have distinctive swing styles, yet , there may be certain movements and positions that can be adjusted so that we, too, can **enhance** our own golf game. Listed below are the shared habits of the pros. Recognizing and adopting them can be of great benefit to you.

1. They maintain a firm grip throughout the golf swing.
2. They have a deliberate and low take away motion and a very good arm extension.
3. Their arms remain away from the body in their upward motion but upon its downward motion, the right elbow (left for lefties) is tucked into the side of the body.
4. As the weight is shifted to the left leg, it allows the arms to straighten out and the wrist to flex back at impact.
5. They maintain a fixed level head position throughout the swing.
6. They have a high finish with good arm extension.

I'm quite sure that the fellow who invented this pastime activity did not have a set of instructions immediately at hand. As this pastime began to catch on, it took on a new meaning and evolved into what it is today. I'm also sure that the originator never thought that it would turn out to be a world wide sport played by so many people. And, I'm pretty sure that the first golf swing didn't resemble the swing of today's pros.

Perfecting a golf swing like that of the 'Iron Byron' would be ideal but to do that we, too, would have to be a machine. Unfortunately, we are not machines or robots, nor are we perfect. Therefore, we cannot expect to hit perfect straight shots each and every time. We can, however, use the mechanical Iron Byron as a model from which to learn the proper execution of a golf swing.

When I speak of a golf swing, I mean a swing that is specifically designed to hit a golf ball. A baseball swing or a tennis swing is not a golf swing. A simulation of chopping wood or a swing that makes you look as though you were screwing yourself into the ground is not a golf swing. I'm not asking that you develop a perfect swing but to develop a swing that can give you a reasonable golf shot. A swing that is good enough to hit the ball with authority and purpose. As you may have noticed, many pros do not have the **prettiest** looking swings, however, they get the job done and that's what counts.

Beginners should learn the proper golf swing in sequence. Some books depict the swing in graphs like the one illustrated below. This, at least, gives you an overall mental image of the swing. Whether left handed or right, each of these lines represent the club positions. The lines with the arrows correspond to the end of your backswing and the finish of your total golf swing. Again, whether you are left handed or right, you will notice in the graph that the legs are not apart. Some use this as a starting position and then **separate** the feet to adjust to a more comfortable stance.

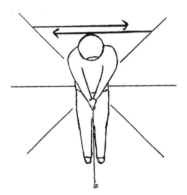

Balance, practice, repetition, co-ordination and application, along with a will to learn, are the combinations needed to develop a good golf swing. Give yourself time. After all, Rome wasn't built in a day as the old saying goes. Since golf is not a game that comes naturally to one, it requires effort and a stick-to-it determination. Avoid negative thoughts. Feeding your mind with thoughts like "I can't do it", "I'll never learn", "It's too difficult" or "I'm hopeless" is suicidal golf. Substitute instead phrases like "I can do it", "I will do it" and "I know I can do it". Think positive. Sow seeds of optimism.

When, after much practise, you see the ball doing what you want it to do, you're going to say "By George, I think I've got it". Then, it's just a matter of repeating your own swing style, your trademark.

Whittle away at learning the golf swing. At home, practice the set-up and grip alignment. You will reap the rewards of your labor if you don't give up. Then you, too, will have something in common with the pros.

CHAPTER **20**

IT HAPPENS TO THE BEST

You are not alone! No one has exclusivity when it comes to hitting an errant golf shot. Most of us have experienced those days when we should have stayed home rather than play golf. There are days when everything we do in golf goes right. Then we have those days when, well, you know, when everything goes wrong. You are not alone. Welcome to heartbreak golf.

Bad games deflate us. We shake our heads in disgust and lose sight of the fun. It's demoralizing. Tell me, why should we discourage ourselves? How can we make the most of a bad situation?

First, we can take solace in the knowledge that experiencing bad days also happens to the best. At a senior's skins game held in Maui, Hawaii, 1996, the great Jack Nicklaus shanked a shot! Dottie Mockrie took a seven on a par four hole playing against the seniors and P.G.A. players. Mental errors. Long ball hitting John Daly bogeys par fives. Tom Watson finally wins a tournament after 9 years! The list goes on.

Who would have thought that Gregg Norman, who was leading the 1996 Masters by six strokes, would lose to Nick Faldo by five shots. You and I can only speculate as to what happened but only Gregg knows that answer. Take solace Gregg, Arnold Palmer had a seven stroke lead on Billy Casper with nine holes to go in the 1966 U.S. Open. Casper tied Palmer and went on to win the Open. This had to have brought back memories for Arnold.

There will be many more stories yet to be told. We are all human and it happens to the best of players.

The pros play every week, year in and year out, and still make mental errors. So, if you are only a week-end golfer, why do you expect perfection when you, yourself, are not perfect? Have you ever noticed that when you make an errant shot, you get upset? Then, you compound that errant shot with your emotional frustration and execute another errant shot? Many pros fail to qualify for the last rounds of tournament play. It can be very disheartening to miss qualifying by one stroke. How many times have you seen the front runners take the gas in the closing holes? Tom Kite, on his first major tournament at Pebble Beach, didn't play picture perfect golf. He scrambled and scrambled well.

Observe how many greenside bunkers the pros play out of. An errant shot caused the ball to end up in the bunker. Nobody thinks about that. All they say is, "Oh, he'll get out and make his par. No sweat".

Golf commentators are provided with stats on each player. They know at a glance exactly where any given player stands on the list of the most consistent ball strikers, hitting fairways and greens, how many putts they average per round, how many sandies etc. It's interesting and surprising to know at what rank each pro stands. The weekly tournament produces only one winner and only his name will stand out and be remembered unless, of course, he commits a **catastrophic** blunder in which case he, as the loser, will be remembered. As a result of Greg Norman's stunning loss at the Masters in 1996, he unwittingly made himself infamous. He will always be remembered by catch phrases like 'pulling a Norman' or 'pulled a Norman' when similar circumstances arise.

Blunders, errant shots and mishits will continue to happen, even to the best, so take comfort in knowing that you are not alone when it comes to errant shots.

One lady who used to travel a lot on her own was asked by my wife if she was ever afraid of travelling alone and getting lost. Her answer, "I never get lost, I just find new places". She turned a negative into a positive. A lesson can be learned from this intrepid lady. Whenever you make an errant shot, you're going to find yourself in a new situation, a new experience. Make the most of a bad situation and turn it into a positive.

Let's say you're not hitting the driver well. Switch over to another club, a three wood or a three iron. All is not lost if only you refuse to give up. Keep in mind that the sun does not shine everyday. Whatever you do, never give up on yourself. Think of ways to get your game on track, check your set-up, grip and alignment. Check your attitude. What's distracting you? Is there something at home? Or, at work? Maybe you're working on a problem and you're trying to solve it on the golf course. Think! Mental preparedness plays a major role in the outcome of your golf game.

When all systems fail, play golf as though you're just practicing. Think of ways to do positive things with your game. Refuse to give up. Think positive and think of your errant shots as a **new** experience. Remember, it happens to the best. Try **laughing** at yourself, it helps!

CHAPTER **21**

STROKE SAVERS

A stroke saved is a stroke earned... Dan Kirby

The countless number of strokes needlessly squandered by golfers is mind boggling. This happens when little or no thought is given on HOW to save strokes. Saving strokes on your game means better scores and more fun and, next to fun, saving strokes should be your prime concern. A bad swing or our golf equipment usually takes the rap for our mistakes. Following are a few stroke savers to help shave your score.

Do you get the 1st hole jitters? This is where many golfers put themselves behind the 8 ball. Here we get to see every conceivable shot there is to be made: a pop up, a dribble, a complete miss, a push or pull to mention but a few. There are oodles of strokes sacrificed on the very first tee. How can we save strokes? The key word is 'relax'. Loosen up, do some stretching, swing a few clubs. **Avoid** forcing your swing. Pick a target and swing as though you are practising. A relaxed frame of mind can do wonders.

At one time or another, we're all guilty of this next stroke stealer. It's the 'peek-a-boo' or 'heads up' golf. This is caused by our being overly anxious about where our ball is going to land. We lift our heads too quickly resulting in blooping or sculling the shot. So, how can we save strokes? If you are going to run or lob a shot, pick a target, plan your shot, keep your head still and follow through. **Never quit on your execution.** This is tough to do but worth it as it means saving strokes.

Indecision is another stroke stealer. Saving strokes here is a bit tricky because a lot depends, believe it or not, on the weather. The best advice that I can give you here is to know your yardage and execute the swing without hesitation. This is no time to have two thoughts - maintain one thought as any hesitation on your part will result in a mis-hit. He that hesitates is lost!

The main culprit to stroke loss that I see time and time again is **uncontrolled emotions.** A golfer mis-hits a shot and gets angry with himself. His 'loose' emotions gets the best of him and without thinking clearly, compounds one mis-hit upon another. He shoots a 13 on a par 3. I have seen this happen with my own eyes. Why does this happen? **Uncontrolled emotions!** To save strokes in this situation, meaning a bad putt or a mis-hit, back away. Regroup. Now is not the time to cry over spilled milk nor let stupidity get the best of us but a time to save strokes so, instead of being upset, bring down your blood pressure. Settle down your thoughts and focus. Remember golf doesn't beat you, you beat yourself. A good flexible game plan will result in saving strokes. Demanding **perfection** of yourself is not reasonable. No one but no one executes a perfect shot every time. Learn to be patient with yourself, enjoy your game, the weather and some good company. Giving thought to saving strokes should always be at the back of your mind.

Maintain your cool, settle down and avoid making matters worse. Remember, a stroke saved is a stroke earned.

CHAPTER **22**

CLUBMAKERS

BUYER BEWARE! is the consumer group's motto and with good reason. Here are a few tips to keep in mind when purchasing a set of clubs. Buying brand name clubs does not make you a better golfer. They just want you to think that. There is no need to spend $1500.00 to $2000.00 for a set of clubs unless, of course, you have money to burn. I've had a 1959 set of Walter Hagen's since 1964 and paid $35.00 for them. They have served me well to this day! But, then again, that's me. When a salesperson pressures you to buy a set of clubs or tells you that the clubs in your hands are perfect for you, stop and think. If those clubs were made for you, then what are they doing sitting on the rack waiting to be sold to someone else?

A schooled clubmaker would be your best bet when you're ready to purchase a proper set of clubs. Why? Because he can custom fit them for you, make them to your specifications. It's the difference between buying a suit off the rack or having it taylor-made to fit you exactly. A person behind the counter is not a clubmaker, he's there to sell merchandise.

Any Tom, Dick or Harry can change a grip or a shaft. Beware! He may not know what he's doing. For instance, does he know that changing the grip or the shaft will affect the playability of a club? Does he know that it will affect the swing weight? If he says it doesn't matter, move on. That's a clue telling you he lacks knowledge and experience.

Too many beginners and unsuspecting golfers get the merry-go-round treatment, when after buying a set of clubs, find they can't play with them. They are advised to take lessons. A number of lessons later, they still can't play with their new clubs. After much wasted time and a lot of money has changed hands, they are left in limbo. No one seems to know what is wrong. The teacher blames the student and the student blames the teacher. The student has to be correct.

There are many errant and/or inconsistent golf shots. An area that is almost totally overlooked as a probable cause is the lie angle of the club. The majority of golfers are not aware that due to their position, they create for themselves an upright lie or a flat lie with their clubs. The following illustrations demonstrate three lie angles.

LIE ANGLES

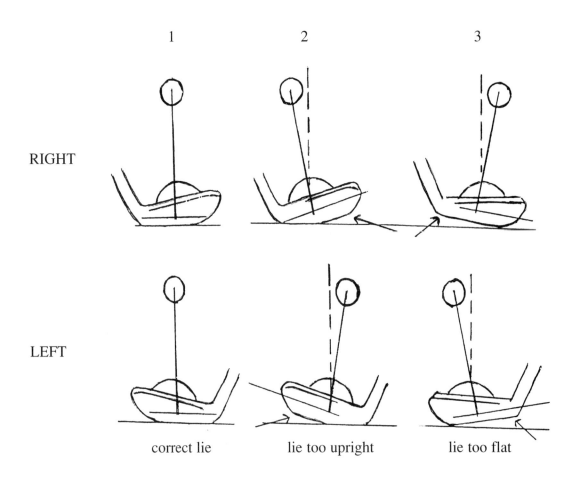

1	2	3

RIGHT

LEFT

correct lie   lie too upright   lie too flat

Club #1   shows us the correct lie position. When you have the correct lie, and hit the ball squarely, you should have a relatively straight shot.

Club #2   has a lie angle that is too upright. Your ball, as the illustration shows, will go left. (right for left-handers) This clubhead lie would be ideal for an uphill lie where the ball is above one's feet.

Club #3   has a lie that is too flat. The ball will go right (left for lefties) this lie angle would be ideal for a downhill lie or when the ball is below one's feet.

NOTE: The following illustration of the intended flight of the ball under certain lie conditions.

Illustrations below show flight of ball under lie situation.

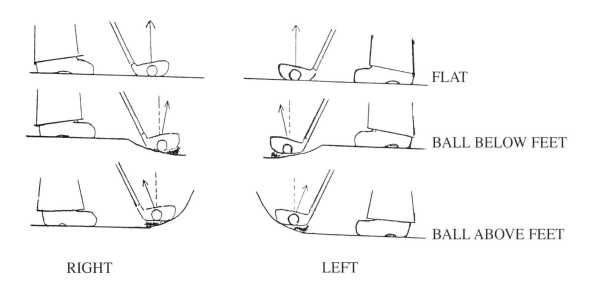

FLAT

BALL BELOW FEET

BALL ABOVE FEET

RIGHT   LEFT

Golfers are not aware that their height and length of arms will either create an upright lie or a flat lie. Clubs that are constantly used and abused will need to have the **loft and lie** checked now and then. Any adjustments to be made should be done by a clubmaker who has the 'loft and lie machine'. This procedure takes time, so be patient. It will save you a lot of money, as well as give you a better game of golf.

More golfers should consider having their clubs checked for the loft and lie angle before chucking them out to buy a whole new set. Advertising tells us that we need to invest in a new set of clubs in order to correct our problems. It may not be necessary at all. Do a little investigating first. Otherwise, you may find yourself with a brand new set of clubs AND the same problem. Advertising and the mind. What a combination!

Many golfers are under the impression that the shaft is the ultimate answer to good golf. Well, I disagree. You may have the best shafts in the world installed on your clubs but if your lie angle is too upright or too flat, your best shaft will not correct your problem. There is no question that good shafts make a difference but it isn't the number one cure-all. There are too many variables to be considered.

When golfers have a lie problem, they unknowingly adjust the club with each swing. If you do have a problem, search for a certified clubmaker, explain your problem and have him check your clubs. You may find that you save a bundle of money and save your clubs to boot.

Why is the driver difficult to hit? Take your five iron and place it alongside your driver. Now, compare and note the difference. First of all, the driver is longer. Secondly, the face angles are different and thirdly, the loft and lie are also different. Common sense will tell you that hitting a ball from these two clubs will differ dramatically.

This subject matter is technical but bear with me. I'll only highlight why the driver is difficult to hit. Aside from the length of the driver, the 'hosel bore' which is the neck of the driver could be misbored or off center thereby creating a slice or hook angle. The horizontal face bulge along with the center of gravity are other factors that need to be considered. I bring this to your attention because you may have a good swing and yet experience directional problems. Drivers come in **open, square** and **closed** faces and in various degrees. This is where an experienced clubmaker can come to your rescue.

All too often we finger the golf swing or the shaft as the culprits when we have a bad golf game so consider the loft and lie of your club as well as the face angle. When it comes to the golf swing and golf equipment, there are many variables that need consideration. See your local club doctor.

For any technical assistance and clubmaking, you can contact

Golfsmith: 1-800-925-7709
Dynacraft: 1-800-942-5872
The Golfworks: 1-800-848-8358
U.T. Golf: 1-800-708-7767

CHAPTER

THE GOLF SWING

A golf swing is like a finger print. No two are alike. Even though a person may have been taught to swing a golf club, he will ultimately develop a trademark style of his own. Our individual personalities, mannerisms and idiosyncrasies are what identify us. Likewise with our golf swing. Our buddies recognize us by our certain stance, our off-beat swing, our grip position or peculiar finish. Whatever it may be, these are our trademarks and it identifies us. I remember a fellow golfer who would literally bounce the shaft of the club off the back of his head when he used his driver or lower irons.

The important element you want to remember about the golf swing is; make sure the clubhead returns **square** to the ball at impact! Your take off and landing is crucial.

Moe Norman, a Canadian professional, has a swing that would have you in total disbelief and yet he is the straightest ball striker in North America or, for that matter, the world. Viewed by today's golf teaching standards, Moe **defies** all the teaching methods and breaks the rules on how to hit a golf ball. His wide stance would automatically catch your attention. His grip position is unconventional in the way that he places his thumb on the shaft. His arms are stretched out well away from his body and the clubhead is about twenty inches behind the ball. You would swear that with this type of set-up, he could never hit the ball straight.

Moe remains flat-footed until after striking the ball and then this right heel rises. His back swing motion is slow and deliberate. His swing looks to be executed in one motion but his wrists flex allows his upward swing motion to reach its maximum. Moe makes a sweeping-like motion as he makes contact with the ball, with his arms well stretched out. Moe has his own particular trademark at the end of his swing. He returns the club forward and points it skyward. As off-beat as his swing may be to onlookers, he holds over thirty golfing records. They say that there's an exception to every rule and Moe Norman is definitely that. The artist's conception of his swing is illustrated.

Shown below are just three swing variations. Note the different stances, different club and head positions. They have different points of wrist flexing, different club positions and lengths of upward swing motion. Compare one spectrum of the backswing from one golfer to another. Pictured is the artist's conception of the backswings of John Daly, Doug Sanders and my son, Kariwate. Who is to say how far back one should extend the golf club. **To each his own.** What may work for one may not work for another. If you want to compare one spectrum of one golf swing to another, simulate the swings of Doug Sanders and John Daly.

#1   John Daly's backswing is extended beyond the norm.
#2   This is my conception of Doug Sander's 3/4 backswing
       Notice the vast difference between his and John's
#3   My son keeps his club position parallel

Interestingly, Doug Sanders missed a short putt to win the British Open while John Daly sunk a long putt to win the British Open. This information only goes to show that there is no one particular swing that makes **champions**. Every golf shot does not require the same stance, club or execution. The pros do not execute every shot perfectly. There are too many variables to consider. The **more** moving parts you have in anything, the **more** chance of it breaking down. Note the illustration below to see what the golf swing entails from start to finish. What are the chances of something going wrong in a golf swing? Plenty!

The golf swing hinges on one's health, height, weight, age, physical fitness and abilities. Knowing our handicaps and limitations and playing within those limitations have to be seriously considered. If you are satisfied with your swing and it works for you, **stay with it** and have fun. Ignore people who think they know what's best for you. Usually, these types who are ever ready to give advice, rarely, if ever, take their own.

DiMarco has hot putter Grabs Quebec Open lead with "funky" grip. This was the headline news that splashed on the sports page of the Gazette in Montreal Aug. 18 1996.

American Chris DiMarco was attributing his good scores to a "funky" grip. His comments were "It looks funky, but it works." "At least it works for me." So no matter if you have an unusual swing, grip, stance etc. if it works for you **STAY WITH IT.**

CHAPTER **24**

LEARN TO LEARN IN FUN

Do you know of anyone who does not take pleasure in fun? Fun is always associated with children at play. They have this innocent quality and state of mind that makes their learning process fun. Their minds are **void** of pressure, tension and anxiety. They're worry free. Childrens' minds are like sponges readily absorbing information with an amazing ability to adapt and adjust. Children do not learn games for the sake of 'competing' with other children. To children, learning is fun, new experiences are fun. As adults, we can take a lesson from children when it comes to learning in fun.

The word 'fun' is too freely used and only loosely associated with golf. When people learn to play golf for the sole purpose of beating or besting their friends, they lose out on the fun and enjoyment that this game has to offer. After all, fun does not breed frustration, anxiety and disappointment. Competition does. Fun is supposed to relieve us of stress and tension.

Competition is practically unavoidable in this day and age but can we not find a balance between competition and fun? There are never any happy losers because it's just no fun to lose.

How many activities can you cite in which you had fun while you learned? Driving a car, learning to swim and ski and probably even learning how to cook would be a few of those activities.

Do you remember the times when you tried to cook and burnt the meal or maybe it didn't come out the way it was supposed to? Did you try to burn the house down or beat up your stove? Of course not. It was trial and error but you eventually learned and today everyone looks forward to your apple pie!

When it comes to golf, learning in fun means keeping your emotions under control. That control will prevent you from displaying poor sportsmanship and bad conduct. Learning in fun means that if you mis-hit a shot you don't throw your club, break your club or pound your club in disgust. No, you **laugh** it off and go on.

The synonym of fun is enjoyment and enjoyment means taking pleasure in whatever activity in which we engage ourselves.

One of the main culprits that deprive us the full enjoyment of the golf game is **stress.** Unconsciously, we carry stress to the golf course thereby affecting the pleasure that the game has to offer. To combat this culprit, we need to develop a new attitude, a new outlook to the purpose of this sport. We need to learn how to derive that pleasure.

After a day at work, especially if our job is stressful, what do we want to do? Relax! We certainly don't want to carry it with us into leisure time. Since fun means enjoyment, we need to learn to enjoy, to find the pleasure in golf. It is, afterall, a recreational sport. **No** enjoyment means **no** fun.

Learning in fun is made easier when you understand yourself and have respect for the game. The ABC's of Golf will aid you to approach the game with a different, lighter perspective and will show you that learning in fun helps you to do the best you can. It means having a relaxed frame of mind, free from worry and pressure.

There are more important things in life than golf so why take this game so seriously, especially if you don't have to make a living playing golf. Life is short enough. There's no need to make it harder for ourselves. We don't have to solve the world's problems so why not just enjoy and have fun?

Learn to learn in fun and enjoy.

CHAPTER **25**

THE LEARNING ATTITUDE

In my golf school, a sign is mounted for everyone to see and read. One quote is from the late gum chewing, rope trick artist and humorist Will Rogers. He once said, "The more I travel, the more I meet people, the more I realize how little I know." The other is mine. "Learning is like space, there is no end."

A human interest story out of Dallas, Texas, tells of a man who is just now learning how to read at the age of ninety. His circumstances prevented him from attending school as a youngster. His streetwise (common sense) answer to why he's learning how to read at this late age caught my interest. "**A wise man will change, a fool will not.**" Basically, he summed up my subject about the learning attitude. There are two distinct lessons we can learn from him and his answer. One is that no one is ever too old to learn, so we can throw that most used excuse out the window. Secondly, he has the learning attitude.

Scientists are now discerning that physical exercise and learning stimulate the brain cells, inactivity of these cells cause a breaking down and eventual uselessness. The brain requires oxygen and food. This food is knowledge, forever learning.

What is required to have this learning attitude? First, let's consider the tools that we have available to learn with. We learn through the senses of hearing, sight, smell, taste, touch and the sense of heat in our skin. We learn by example, oral and written instruction, past experience, trial and error, insight and understanding, practice and challenging recreational activities.

Since golf is both challenging and creative, the will or desire to learn has to be there. A desire stimulates interest and enthusiasm. Desires have also been known to be short-lived, so **determination** and a **stick-to-it** attitude are contributing factors in having the learning attitude. A learning attitude is a hunger or craving for knowledge and that hunger needs to be satisfied. The brain needs oxygen and food, brain food, information.

When we're asked to think matters over, it's food for thought. The National Enquirer is known by its catchy phrase, "Inquiring minds want to know". This gossip 'food' though is not healthy for the mind, yet people crave to know the latest gossip. It's that hunger to know that needs to be satisfied. Satisfy your hunger for golf and you'll learn.

When I ask you to use your imagination, I'm asking you to draw upon your knowledge and experience and associate it to your golf swing. Ask yourself, "What does this remind me of?" For instance, to me, the baseball stance is similar to the golf stance. The timing of hitting either the baseball or golf ball too early or too late will have similar results. One ball going to the left or to the right. This association is a valuable aid in understanding and executing the golf swing.

After learning the 'set-up', learn the golf swing in sequence. We learned our alphabetical letters in order and our numbers in sequence. Learn to understand the golf swing and, like the juggler, learn to co-ordinate the swing from the beginning to the finish. Allow time for your learning to take root. **Impatience impedes growth.** They say that you learn easier and better when you take short practice sessions. Remember to incorporate your own ideas. It's your swing.

Learning to set realistic goals that are attainable eliminates any unnecessary pressure and tension. Avoid negative thoughts and negative attitudes as they produce negative results. It was Benjamin Franklin who said, "Example is the best teacher." Playing golf with advanced golfers will improve your game. There's no doubt whatsoever to the truth of those words.

Learning means making adjustments. Whether you realize it or not, we make adjustments every day. Our schedules are altered due to weather, health, accidents and unforeseen occurances. We think nothing of making these adjustments, yet we're reluctant to make adjustments to a weak area in our swing. Playing golf over the years has cemented golf swings either for the good or for the bad. Continually using a bad swing serves only to reinforce it. This is where the learning attitude comes in and this is when students say, "I took golf lessons but I was never informed about making the most out of **my** swing."

Aside from this story, adjusting is the key word to a better golf swing so learn to adjust. Learn to believe in yourself and not get down on yourself. Learn from your mistakes and correct them.

We all learn from one another, even out of the mouths of babes, so to speak. Never feel embarrassed to ask questions. Adopt a learning attitude and you'll be surprised and amazed to see how much you can learn - and be happier for it.

NO ONE PERSON KNOWS IT ALL AND NO ONE PERSON EVER WILL.

CHAPTER **26**

CHANGE OR ADJUSTMENT? WHICH?

The word 'change' can have a rebellious effect on some individuals. A wall of resistance is met by those intruders who persist in changing people. "Nobody is going to change me" is their attitude.

You must agree that certain changes are advantageous and for our betterment. For instance, a change of weather is a welcome relief. A vacation is a change from our daily routine. When the tires on our car are in bad condition, a change is mandatory for our personal safety as well as the safety of others. Can you think of changes you personally benefitted from? Isn't it ironic that people who resist change are often the ones who change their minds in everyday decisions?

There are things that do not need changing, just an adjustment. We adjust our television sets. We adjust the heat on our stove and we adjust the lights by pushing the dimmer switch. Do you have an adjustable wrench in your tool box? When they tune up your car, they don't change the carburator. They adjust the idle screw. To adjust means to adapt. When we adapt, we want to 'fit in' to the situation or circumstances.

As a golf teacher, I believe that it is not only wrong to change a person's golf swing, it's a waste of time. One of the drawbacks to teaching is that most students, whether beginners or advanced, always **revert** back to their old swings eventually. Old habits die hard. Adjustments take time. Therefore, patience and a stick-with-it attitude and practice will make your adjustment become second nature. Most golfers are not going to be professionals and advanced golfers need only a pat on the back for reassurance or - a minor adjustment.

Swing change is not the answer to many golfers' problems. Learn the basics of golf and note where you need to make adjustments. No one has a perfect golf swing even though some may think they have. Keep in mind your abilities and physical strengths. Avoid doing anything that will do more harm than good.

INTRODUCTION TO

The following pages deal with the ABC's of golf. The information and illustrations presented are at least a starting point. Carefully go through the material and review it. Remember, nothing is **dogmatic.** Take notes, extract only what is useful to you. Incorporate your own thoughts and ideas because the golf swing is yours and yours alone. Maintain your self identity.

Every golfer needs to acquaint himself with the ABC's of golf as these are what make the strong basic foundation on which you need to build.

The golf SET-UP consists of the **grip**, the **posture**, the **ball position** and the **alignment**. This is your substratum on which all other future golf knowledge will rest.

Once again, I am going to encourage you to use your imagination when considering this information and be innovative when using it.

Above all things, stay with what works for YOU.

CHAPTER **27**

THE SET-UP

The answer to people's problems is sometimes right under their very noses. They just can't smell it. For instance, people want to learn to play golf properly. The way to do that is to get to know the basics, the 'set-up'. The set-up is the ABC's or substratum on which the XYZ's of golf will rest on.

To get the maximum from your golf swing, you need to position yourself or set yourself up properly. An improper set-up will create an unbalanced swing. **Balance,** then, is the key to a good set-up.

Three illustrations are provided depicting the set-up. We will consider them individually and extract the main points. The set-up involves the **grip, posture, ball position** and **alignment.** These illustrations are a starting point to help you on your way. Starting on the right foot in any endeavor insures the best possible results. There is nothing that says you must conform to these models. There are oodles of positions and variations other than what you see here but avoid letting it disturb or confuse you. You, yourself, will in due time, develop your own unique style or trademark.

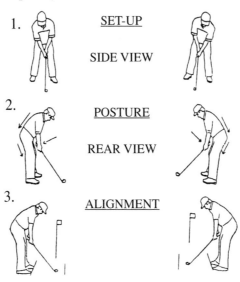

1. SET-UP
   SIDE VIEW

2. POSTURE
   REAR VIEW

3. ALIGNMENT

The models are depicting the set-up holding a 5 iron.

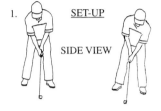

Illus. #1   shows us the side view
   a.   hands are positioned near the inner thigh
   b.   ball position just off left center
   c.   stance is shoulder width
   d.   shoulder is tilted slightly downward

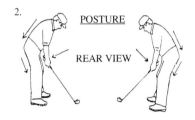

Illus. #2   posture-rear view
   a.   bent at 45° degree angle
   b.   knees flexed
   c.   hands at least 6" from body

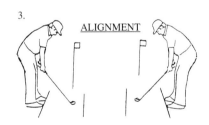

Illus. #3   alignment
         body, hands, feet and club
         aligned towards intended target

Since the set-up requires balance, proper weight distribution is a must. Find your comfortable position making sure that your weight is **evenly** distributed. Avoid getting technical, there's no need to aim for perfection. Keep on reviewing this material every now and then as a reminder of your proper set-up.

POSTURE

Do you know why a flamingo stands on one leg? Because, if he didn't he would fall down. Like a flamingo, good body posture means balance. Bad posture indicates that the body is not properly aligned. This alignment, proper or improper, will affect the rest of the body. It even affects our personalities.

1.

POSTURE

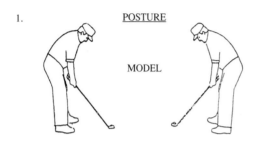

MODEL

1.   Maintaining proper posture as model #1 is showing, will ensure the required balance.

2.

2.   The knees are too bent. Golf is not played in a sitting position and the hands are too close to the body.

3.

RIGHT   LEFT

3.   No knee flex. Distribute your weight, some have too much weight on their toes and others on their heels. Balance your weight.

Illustrations 2 and 3 are not in balance. As a result, they will sacrifice the maximum power potential needed from the body, arms and legs. The solution is obvious. #2 has to raise himself up a few inches and position his hands forward. #3 needs only to flex his knees. As they adjust themselves, they will need to adjust their club positions as the lie angle of the club will change. Is this your problem?

ALIGNMENT

We don't generally get around to fixing something unless its broken but sometimes it may be necessary to correct or adjust a given situation or problem. For example, people with poor eyesight would need corrective lenses to ensure better vision or a chiropractor may need to adjust the spine of one who has back problems.

In golf, inconsistent ball flight indicates that an adjustment is in order to rectify the problem. In order to do that, one needs to learn **HOW** to align the body, the hands and the club towards the intended target.

In the illustration below, #2 is our ideal model. The other two are misaligned.

Model #1   This alignment would be for a hooker

Model #3   This alignment is for a big slice, not a controlled fade.

What are the chances of nos. 1 and 3 hitting the target consistently? Not much because as you can see, neither is aimed at the target. Ideally, #2 could pick a **spot** a few feet in front of himself at which to start the ball towards the intended target.

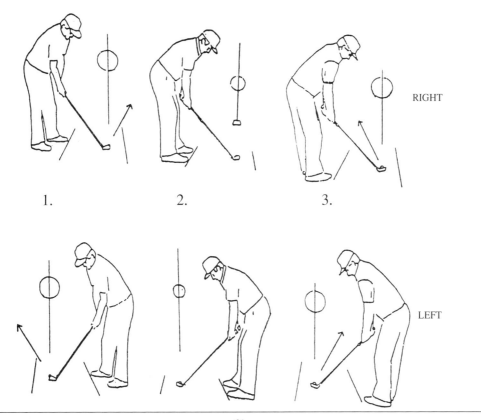

BALL AND CLUB POSITION

Do you have floor tiles? Great! Take a look at the drawing on this page. These squares are actually 12" x 12" floor tiles. These floor tiles will serve as a **perfect** guide for squaring up to the ball and knowing the width of your stance.

Model #1   Shows where the ball and driver should be at address. The ball should be played off the left heel (right for lefties) and the hands placed in the zipper area.

Model #2   Is a 5 iron positioned along one side of the line and the ball on the other. Hands are positioned near the inner thigh.

The illustrations show the different club positions and ball locations of the 5 iron and the driver.

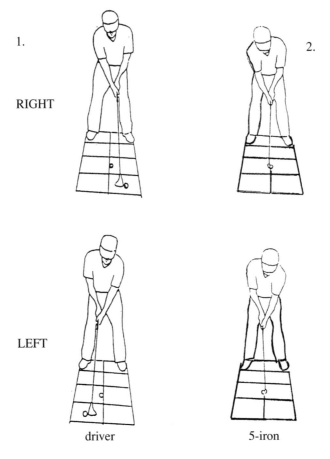

Note the stance. It's neither too narrow nor too wide. Find a balanced stance that is comfortable for you and practise going through the motions without a club. If you have any other ideas, try them and incorporate them into your exercises. **Make it your own.**

HAND POSITIONS

Variety is the spice of life. These words become more evident as we consider the golf hand positions. The illustrations below depict three of the **many** hand positions for the driver.

Model #2   Shows the recommended hand position - at the zipper area.

Model #3   Reminds me of the forward hand position used by Laura Davies in particular. Keep in mind that this is their hand position and it works for them. It doesn't mean that it will work for you.

INSERT (Artist conception of Moe Norman)

Model #1   His hands are more to the rear but not as much as Moe Norman's style. (see insert-artist's drawing) Moe's hand position is like that of model #3 but on the opposite leg. He places his driver about 20" behind the ball. This off-beat looking swing is the straightest ball striker in the world.

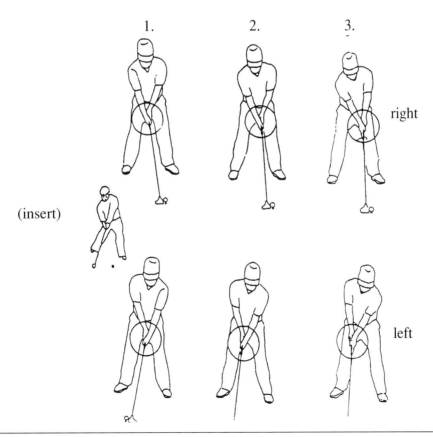

If we split the difference between Moe Norman's hand position and note that of #3, we would get #2, my first suggestion. The reason for this suggestion is that most golfers have a tendency to move their hands **forward** before lifting or taking the club back. This means that #2 would look like model #3 before his lifts his club.

So, next time you're out playing a round of golf and see other hand positions, you shouldn't be surprised. Again, use what makes you feel comfortable and what works for you.

THE GRIP

The phrase 'grip it and rip it' is associated with John Daly. It conveys the need for a strong grip when holding a golf club. When someone says 'Get a grip on life', they're telling you to get your life in order, get it under **control.** These two phrases help me to better understand why a firm grip is necessary. You are in the driver's seat, your grip will control the outcome of your swing and the direction of the ball.

I have chosen to discuss the grip as the last portion of the set-up because of its **importance.** This is the first essential element to better golf. If you are left-handed, you have only to transpose the illustrations to fit them to your needs. The styles of grips and the many variations of finger positions of the hands and the shaft is very intriguing.

As far as I'm concerned, the **most** important thing to learn about the set-up is the grip, all other things being secondary. You will develop feel by and through the grip, through your hands. It is here that you will feel if the ball you hit was solid, weak or just so-so. You are now in control. **Your golf destiny is in your hands.**

If you already have been using a specific grip or are just beginning to develop one, make sure it feels natural. Any discomfort or uneasiness will only offset your swing and game. If you are a beginner, take note of the illustration of the hands. The arrow points to the web between your thumb and forefinger. Some call these the Vs or Ys because of the shape they make. How you position the Vs on the butt end of the club will make a difference to your swing and the direction of the ball. (Compare with page 68).

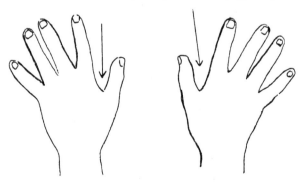

VARIETY OF GRIPS
Pictured here are the 5 grips I have observed through the years.

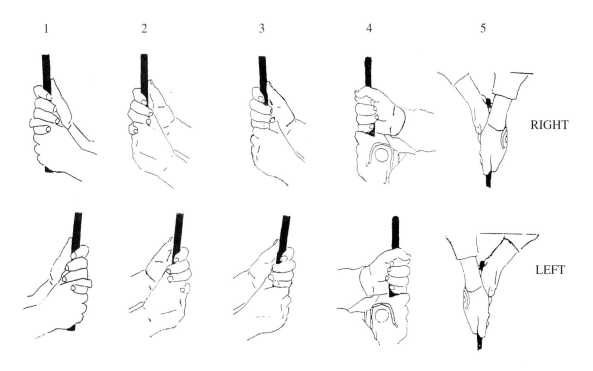

#1   The interlocking grip

#2   The over-lapping grip

#3   The 9-finger grip. (Most people confuse this with the baseball grip.) This is the grip I use. Nine fingers are in a fisted position while the thumb rests on the shaft. This is NOT a baseball grip.

#4   This is the baseball grip. My brother, Herbie, uses this grip. Notice that both hands are in a fisted position. NO thumbs on the shaft. This is the grip I use when I play baseball.

#5   The cross-handed grip. People became familiar with this grip after some pros had difficulty in putting and experimented with this hand position and found it to be effective. It's called this because one hand crosses over the other. It looks like a left handers grip. My brother, Norman, has always used this grip for both baseball and golf. George Cross, whom I mentioned in the beginning, used this grip. Many golfers in my hometown grew up with this type of grip. In fact, we have a CROSS-HANDED, LEFT-HANDED PLAYER! So, when cross-handed putting came into the news, it wasn't new to me.

IMPROPER POSITION OF CLUB IN HAND

Where should we grip a golf club? I want to direct you to the following examples. Follow them step by step as shown.

1. Place your index finger in the middle of your palm
2. Close and squeeze lightly
3. Now, pull out your finger. Note how easily it slid out. This, then, is **not** the right spot to place the club because there is no grip.

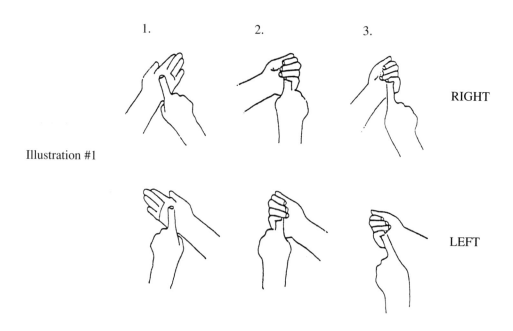

Illustration #1

PROPER POSITION OF CLUB IN HAND

1. Place your index finger at the base of the fingers.
2. Close and squeeze lightly
3. Now pull. Notice the strength and resistance. **This,** then is where your club should be placed. When you squeeze the club in this spot, the butt end will roll onto the padded area of the left hand as shown below.

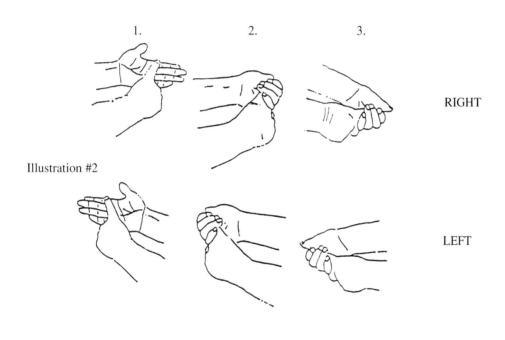

Illustration #2

RIGHT

LEFT

Note : Photo club placement

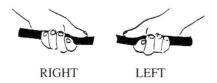

RIGHT   LEFT

PLACING YOUR THUMBS

Illus. #1   Gives you a front view of your grip and the V location
              The thumb is in the 1 o'clock position
Illus. #2   Place your right hand directly over the left hand. The thumb
              should be at the 11 o'clock position as shown above.

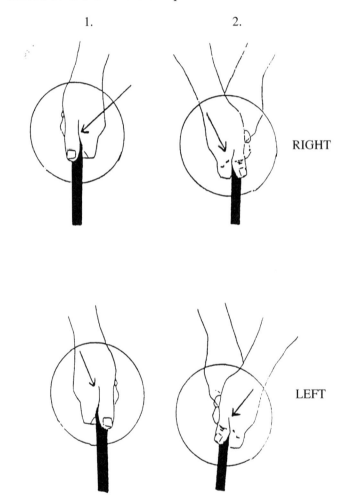

Keep this in mind. The placement of the left thumb on the shaft is at 1 o'clock and the thumb on the right hand is at 11 o'clock. **Reverse for lefties.** Find the hand position that feels natural and comfortable. The following illustration gives more detail.

PLACING YOUR OPPOSITE HAND

Illus. #1 Arrow indicates lifeline

Illus. #2 By placing the lifeline over the thumb of the other hand,
      your grip should look like #3

Illus. #3 This is what your grip should look like. However, you can make any adjustment that is suitable for you as long as you maintain a firm grip.

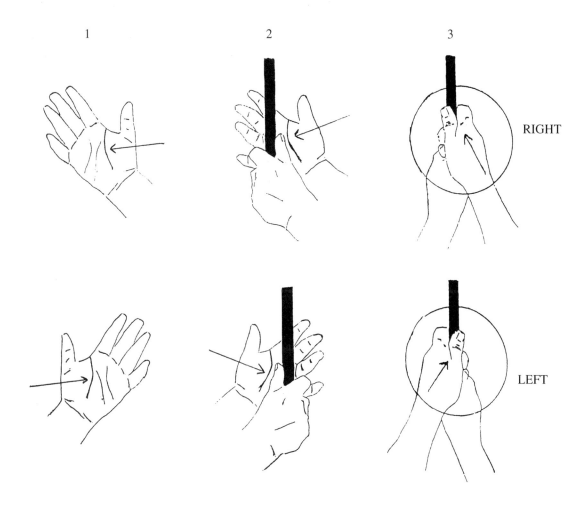

IMPROPER GRIP POSITIONS

Make sure to avoid gripping the club as shown in the next picture. Why?

Illus. #1   Not only is this position not comfortable, it is not conducive to hitting straight shots. The ball will **veer right** because at impact the clubface will be **open.**

Illus. #2   Too much right hand over left you will prevent hitting staight shots. The ball will **veer left** because the clubface will be **closed.** (opposite for lefties)

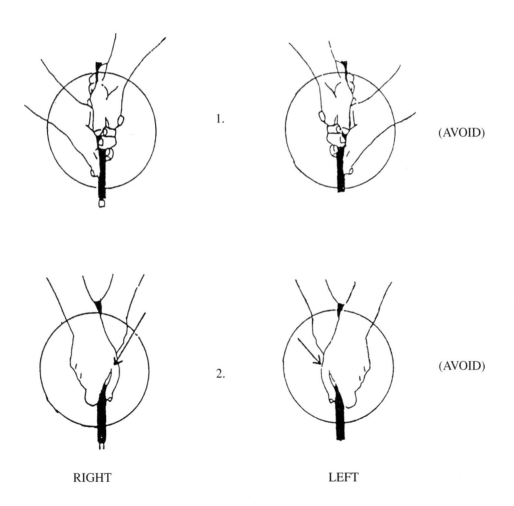

1.

(AVOID)

2.

(AVOID)

RIGHT   LEFT

Below are other variations that golfers use when gripping the club with their left hand. Find the thumb in the 1 o'clock position. 11 o'clock for lefties.

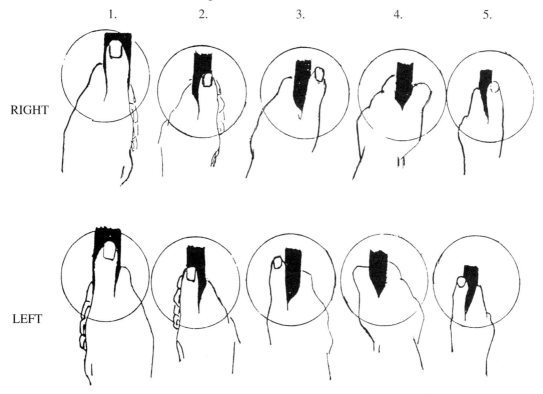

RIGHT

LEFT

GRIP PRESSURE

What is the appropriate grip pressure? Remember, you want and need to stay in control. **Too strong** a grip will cause the hands to pull left, making your ball go left. Finger and thumb indentations on your grip tell you that your grip is too strong. A **too-weak** grip will result in weak shots with the ball going to the right. We want to feel the ball coming off the club. A firm grip is the answer, not too strong, yet, not too weak. Those who have weak wrists and grips and who cannot exercise, because of a physical handicap should try using more club such as woods. A firm grip throughout the swing is CRUCIAL. Trial and error is your best TEACHER.

GRIP SIZES

We all have different hand sizes. Big hands, small hands, fat or thin hands, long or short fingers, etc. Remember, we want to remain in control. Having the proper size grip on our clubs is very important. Golf grips come in different materials and sizes, oversize, undersize, normal as well as grips made for arthritic hands. Along with the many textures, the grips also come in tacky and ultra tacky finishes. We want the size that will **complement** our hands in order to get the best from the club. A good clubmaker should have on stock a set of grips in varied sizes for you to try out. Below is a diagram showing how to judge the correct grip size.

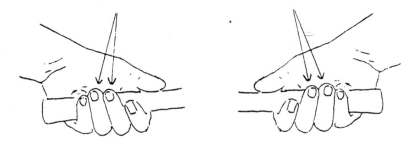

ARROWS INDICATE CHECKPOINTS
RIGHT   LEFT

a. **correct** grip size - when fingers are barely touching thumb pad.
b. grip is too **large** - when fingers are not touching pad
c. grip is too **small** - when fingers DIG into pad

It's easy to do this little test yourself but, if you're still a bit unsure, and need some additional information, your certified clubmaker can help. My recommendation to beginners and to those who have difficulty in holding the club securely is to use the ultra tacky grip. Again it's a matter of preference.

* Hands and wrists need **strength** to handle the work load when playing golf so, strengthening the wrist is essential. Anyone with a weak wrist should think of using lighter weight clubs. Play within your swingweight.

MAINTAINING A FIRM GRIP THROUGHOUT YOUR SWING

As an inventor, I always find that whenever you work on a project, there's always something troublesome that niggles at the back of your mind, something you can't quite put your finger on. That was the case when I was trying to figure out why a number of amateurs were making so many inconsistent golf shots. At one point, these amateurs asked me to have a look at their swings to see if I could determine the cause. On the whole, their swings were okay.

I always knew that a proper grip played a crucial role in executing a golf shot so, at first, I attributed their problems to a weak hand grip. A weak hand grip will cause a twisting of the club in mid-air resulting in a mis-hit. I suggested that they firm up their grip and on doing so, temporarily corrected the problem. However, the problem returned. I took into account the fact that they were not accustomed to using a firmer grip and **reverted** back to their weak hand grips.

Yet, something was still missing. I knew something was wrong.

I experimented with some students just to work out a theory I had. I asked a student to swing a club and I would stop him at certain positions. I did this a number of times just to double check my theory. I was right, but I thought it was an isolated case. However, further testing with other established golfers only confirmed my theory. What caught my eye is captured in the illustration. Their tendency was to open their hand as they take away the club from the body as shown below.

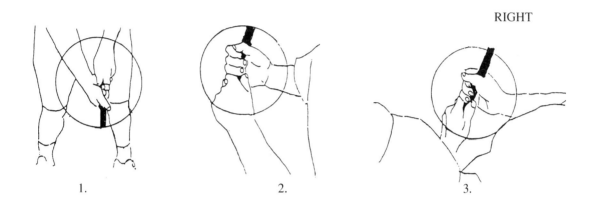

RIGHT

Illus. #1   The hand and grip position
Illus. #2   From the moment the club left the address position, his right hand gradually
   & #3   opened till it reached its upright position. On his downward swing, he closed the right hand. It was like the **opening** and **closing** of a door.

(These are tracings of actual photographs)

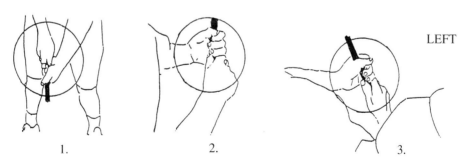

LEFT

You can find out if you have this problem by inserting a pencil between your thumbs and then make your normal swing. If the pencil falls out, it could mean that you need a larger grip or that your hands need to be strengthened by exercise. Ask your golf teacher to watch your hands during your swing. Whatever you do, avoid ignoring the problem. You need to maintain a firm grip throughout your swing. Rectify A.S.A.P.

CHAPTER **28**

LEARNING THE SECRETS OF GOLF

Secrets are like magic, people are mystified and curious. They are in eager anticipation of some revelation to unfold.

Golfers are interested in knowing the secrets of how and what makes the pros so successful. So they're naturally also interested in the latest golf equipment thinking that this might be the key to their success. Take for example this year's hype on titanium drivers. Titanium drivers are not new. They've been around for a while now, just not promoted.

This year, some companies are taking advantage of this hype by selling the titanium driver at a whopping $500.00 to $1000.00. Avoid being fooled. All titanium drivers have the same 6-4 content. (6% aluminum, 4% vanadium, 90% titanium). They want to make a quick buck at your expense.

Your local clubmaker can assemble one for you for under $300.00. For the price on one titanium, you could have two or three made! There is no denying that it is a good club but it will not make you into a better golfer any more than driving a Rolls Royce over a Volkswagen will make you a better driver.

There are no secrets in golf. The secret to any success is **hard work**. All professionals have their own style of swing and there are oodles of variations among them. No two are alike. What I am going to make you aware of is the strengths they have in common. Take note of them, adopt them and put them into practice. Your game will be richly improved.

The comparisons that I'm going to make will help you understand where and what you need to improve on. **I'm only going to highlight crucial areas.** Now that we know the set-up, we can move on to the swinging of the club phase.

The model I'm using is only a visual aid to point out the areas of the swing that need attention. The aim is to learn to take the club back as '**one piece**' and to make a complete follow through in a balanced position. Some golfers assume the position of the model at the outset **then** make their stance position. This is a good idea and a good habit for beginners to get into because you have a position to start from.

Think of these lines as your arms and club extending back and returning to complete the swing. Restricting your arm extension will abort your swing. You want to get the maximum from your arm extension, so **allow** your arms to go free. You will learn how "little things" do mean a lot.

Illustration #1

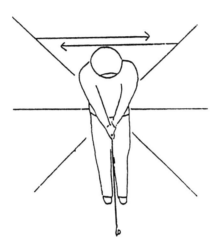

RIGHT   LEFT

 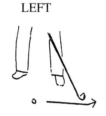

#1 From the address position, we want to take the club back **'low and slow'** to the ground as far as possible and make a gradual incline. By doing this we're developing tempo and arm extension. The pros do this, especially Moe Norman.

RIGHT   LEFT

 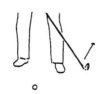

#2 This shows a **common problem** with golfers in the initial stages of the backswing. They raise the club **abruptly** and prevent proper arm extension. Take the club back 'low and slow' **extending** your arms away from the body at the same time.

Illustration #2

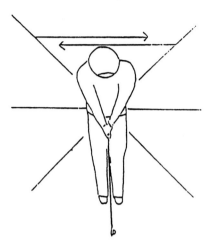

(arm extension)

1.

Model #1

Shows the continual **arm extension** up to the waist. His left knee is bending inward transferring his weight to his right leg. Some use a lot of knee flex, others do not. There is knee action in any case. Player is in balance. Get as much **arm extension** as you can.

Tip: Visualize a friend standing 6' directly behind your swing path and take the clubhead back as though your going to hit his chin. This drill will give you maximum arm extension.

2.

RIGHT   LEFT

Model #2

This golfer has aborted his swing. There is **no arm extension** whatsoever, his wrist has flexed putting him in a **locked** position. The end result would look like he was chopping wood. Player is not in balance.

Illustration #3

As different as the backswings of the pros may be, they have one thing in common - **arm extension.** (these models were posed to duplicate the swings)

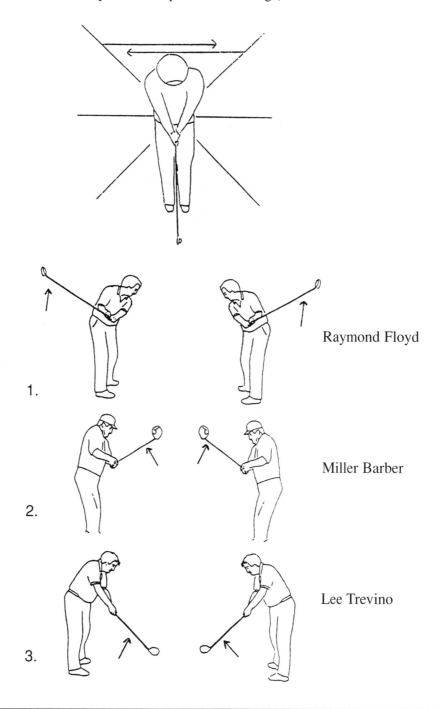

Raymond Floyd

Miller Barber

Lee Trevino

1.

2.

3.

Illustration #4

NOTE ELBOW POSITION

Model #1 a) Right elbow **away** from the body in the upswing.

   b) Knee is flexed

   c) Good arm extension

   d) Good balance.

Note: usually when the left shoulder touches the **chin** area, it indicates sufficient arm extension. Slight variations from golfer to golfer.

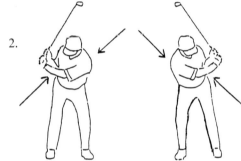

Model #2 a) Right elbow tucked in.

   b) **No** arm extension.

   c) Poor balance.

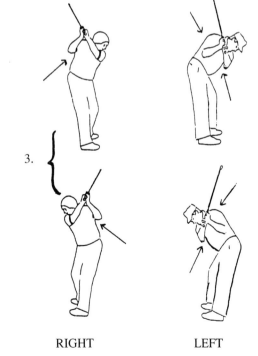

Models in group 3 are **rearview** versions of #1 and #2

Note the arrows.

RIGHT   LEFT

Illustration #5

Model #1 is in a balanced position and ready for the downswing. From the moment you start your back swing, the various body parts begin to 'coil' until it reaches its maximum. From this position (depending how far back you go), you will now begin your down swing or 'uncoiling'. This area is crucial because it is here that your **timing** is set in motion. Remember when I said the more moving parts you have in anything, the more chance of it breaking down? It is here where the body parts, the legs, arms and the body will now have to co-ordinate and synchronize. Any one of these body parts **out of harmony** will throw your timing off. **Too early or too late**, no matter which direction the body is moving, will result in not hitting the ball squarely. How many times have you hit the ball squarely? As simple as this pose looks, there is more to it than meets the eye.

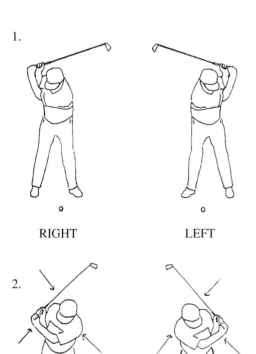

1.

RIGHT   LEFT

Model #1
balanced position - body parts needs to be in sync for good timing.
Too early or too late will cause a mis-hit.

2.

RIGHT   LEFT

Model #2
I'll let you figure out what's not in sync with this swing. Any balance?
How about arm extension? Where are the elbows? Tied up in knots!

Illustration #6

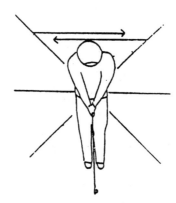

Elbow tucked **in** on downswing

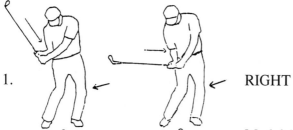

1.   RIGHT

Model #1 All pros and good golfers
    a. Have their elbows **tucked in** on the downswing
    b. Knee flexed and weight transferred to left leg.

2.

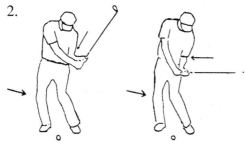

Model #2 Elbows **still** tucked in to his body and has been turning to allow his right arm to straighten out and flex his wrist at impact to finish his timing process.

LEFT

Illustration #7

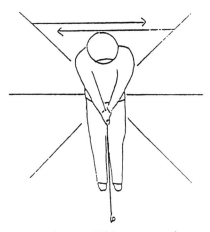

shows us picture #6 in a **rearview** angle

A

B

RIGHT

C

D

LEFT

Model 1   Model 2

Models #1 & #2

A. Elbows tucked in
B. Player in uncoiling position
C. Left arm at target
D. Body turning to allow the arms to straighten out and unleash power

Illustration #8

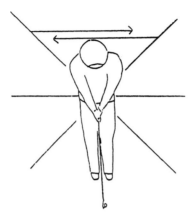

describes **side view** of finish

Model #1 shows his body position

       a.   after impact

       b.   weight is on the left side

       c.   head position remains at same level

Model #2   Does not quit on his execution but follows through

Model #3   A high balanced finish

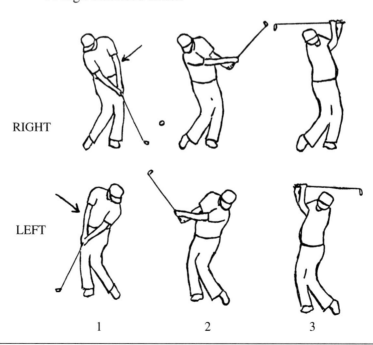

RIGHT

LEFT

       1   2   3

Illustration #9

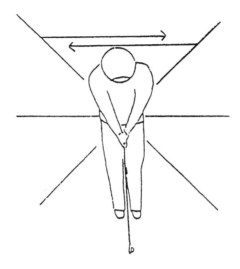

Rearview picture of #8

Model #1   Left arm facing target

Model #2   Final stages of the swing, knee is flexed, weight

Model #3   on the left side and a balanced high finish

RIGHT

LEFT

      1   2   3

Illustration #10

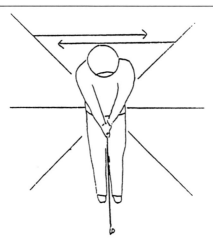

Frontview of picture #9

1.

Elbows tucked in, knee flexed and weight shifting to left leg. Club in horizontal position.

2.

Arms extending straight out at target.

3.

High finish with buckle facing south.

RIGHT   LEFT

Illustration #11

SIDE VIEW

RIGHT

LEFT

REAR VIEW

RIGHT

LEFT

SIDE VIEW AND REAR VIEW OF VARIOUS SEQUENCES

Illustration #12

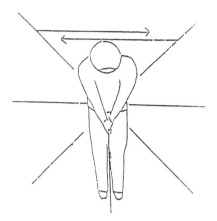

Note & avoid common errors

Model #1   Maintaining level head position throughout the swing makes
                  for balance
Model #2   Unbalance is caused by **raising** the body and head upward.
Model #3   Unbalance is caused by **lowering** the head on the downswing.

A major common problem / a head is bobbing up and down.
Models 2 & 3 - causes "heads up golf" oodles of mis-hits.

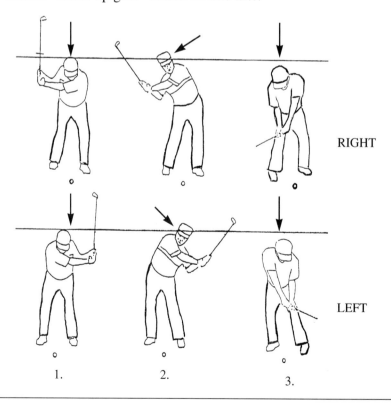

Illustration #13

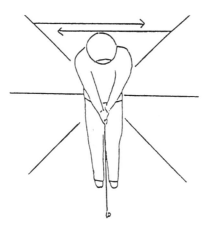

Maintaining **level head** position throughout the swing is another key to good balance.

I cannot emphasize enough how important it is to keep your head **level** throughout your swing. NOTE: How the body is centered and balanced in the illustrations, maintaining a level headed position throughout your swing will improve your golf game.

The body is centered and balanced.

Model #4   Shows us the angled position the head and body should be in after impact.

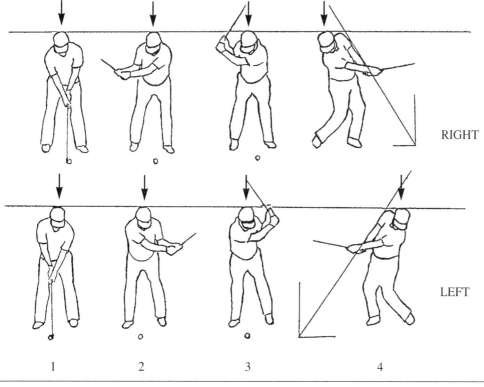

RIGHT

LEFT

1   2   3   4

Illustration #14

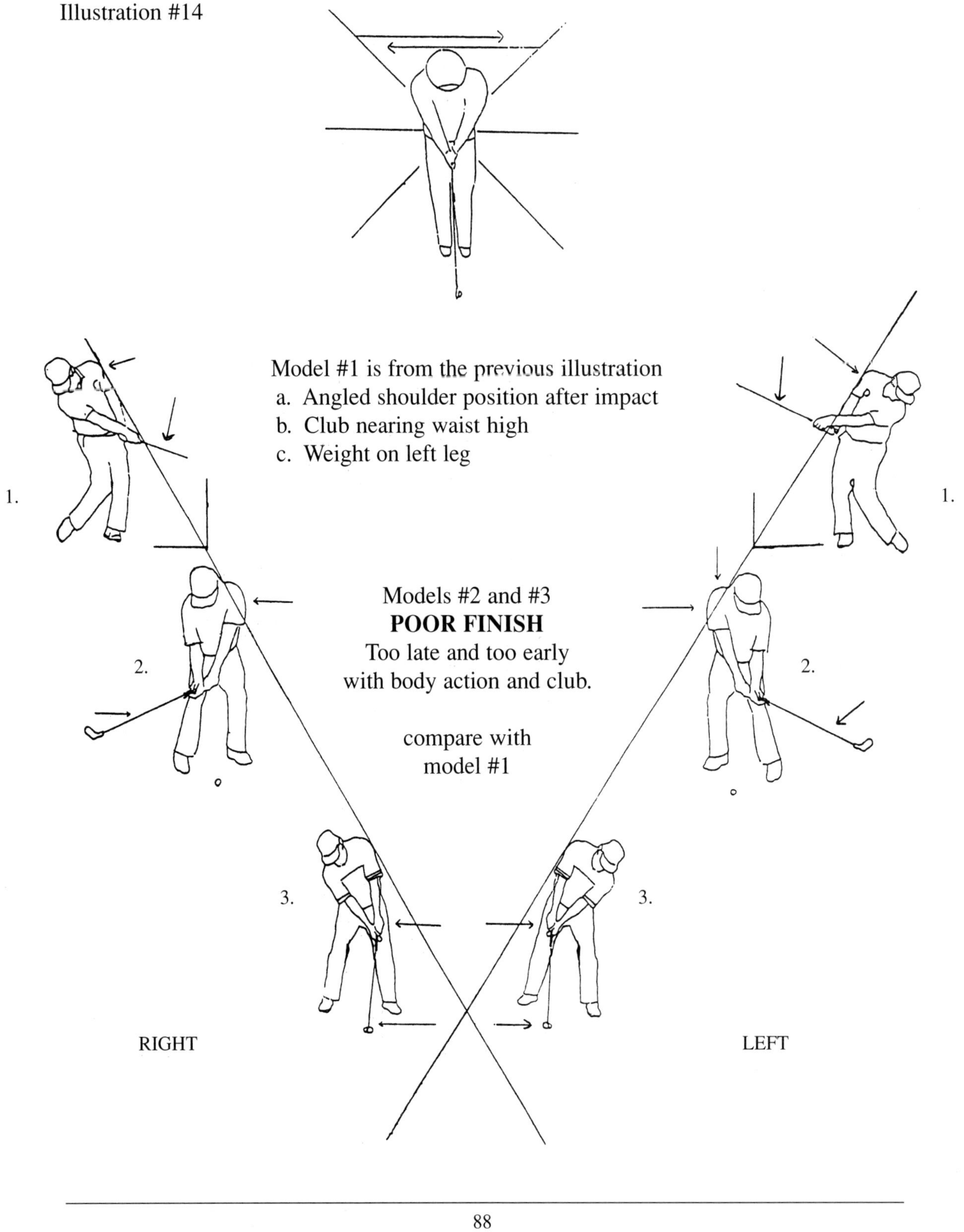

Model #1 is from the previous illustration
a. Angled shoulder position after impact
b. Club nearing waist high
c. Weight on left leg

Models #2 and #3
POOR FINISH
Too late and too early
with body action and club.

compare with
model #1

1.

1.

2.

2.

3.

3.

RIGHT

LEFT

Golfers have a problem with the beginning and the end of the swing.

Illustration #15   **END OF IMPACT**

Model #1   Shows how quickly the club is raised after impact, this aborts the maximum power of your swing. Avoid raising the club too quickly as it causes imbalance.

 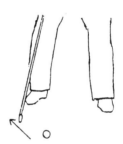

Model #2   Allow the club to pass a foot or so **beyond** the ball in order to use the maximum power of your swing with the full extension of your arms. Avoid quick upward swing!

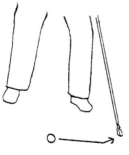 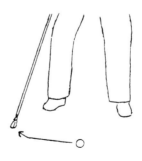

RIGHT   LEFT

KNOWLEDGE IS POWER. Knowing what we know now about the set-up and the common strengths shared by the pros and good golfers, it is within our power to act upon that knowledge.

Knowledge is a building block for improvement and advancement. A little information about the grip, a little information about the posture, a little information about ball position, alignment when assembled together like a puzzle helps us to see the over-all picture of what is needed for a golf swing. The ABC's of Golf is a check list for you to review when you are not playing to **your** level of enjoyment.

Golf knowledge is a requisite in order to play this game properly and well. Your personal contribution of ideas and imagination will greatly enhance your golf knowledge. Never worry about the vast amount of information in the golf world, just remember to adopt and adapt information that is applicable to your situation or circumstance.

We never need to feel that we can over-tax our brains because it has been said that the human brain can contain twenty times the voume of books in the Library of Congress! So. feeding your brain with information will never go to pot - smoking it will.

Acquiring knowledge, sifting information to suit our personal make-up is what we need to focus on. Each person is a separate entity and we need to understand and respect that individuality.

It is impossible for two swings to be identical as the differences of height, weight, age, length of arms and legs, hand size, posture, make this all too evident. This reminds me of a story being told to a roomful of people. Each of those people will **retell** the story with a slightly different spin, having added his own story-telling **touch** or **version.**

We have to make the most of what we have physically, our own natural abilities and the situations presented to us. Practice, playing, the will to learn, the sticking-to-it determination and more practice will pay off in the long run. Just remember that any adjustment to any part of the golf swing takes time and, understandably, will feel awkard at first but, in **due** time, will become second nature to you. Impatience impedes progress. True, learning is not always easy. Understanding doesn't always come naturally but we **cannot** lose sight of the reason we're out there in the first place. We just want to have FUN!

The previous pages deal with the secrets of golf and are merely guidelines for you to consider and/or adopt if you so desire. Learning the secrets of golf ultimately hinges on your personal determination and input. Therefore, the secret to good golfing is playing with better players and personal application.

CHAPTER **29**

COMMON PROBLEMS

Weight transfer – shifting the body weight from one leg to the other in one smooth action is difficult for some golfers to achieve. As easy as this looks, it's a little tricky because you are confronted with those moving parts that need to be co-ordinated and synchronized. This is no small task and it will take many practice drills to find your center of gravity and then learn to stabilize yourself. Like the juggler, balance is the key.

As they begin to take their club away from the address position, many golfers move their bodies as though they have been sucked backwards by a strong vacuum creating a 'bobbing and weaving' effect. **Avoid** the bobs and weaves you are not boxing. Instead, you need to stabilize or maintain control of your body movements and, in so doing, you maintain proper balance and the weight transfer becomes one smooth motion.

The following renderings show but two (#1 & #2) of the many ways to lose your balance. Model #3, however, is centered and balanced. His weight transfer will be smooth.

1. Avoid twisting the body during the golf swing as it will unbalance you.

2. Overextending your body weight forward or backward will also cause imbalance.

3. Proper posture makes for good ablance.

* **Each player needs to find his or her own center of gravity.**

Co-ordinating the arms, legs, hips and waist in the golf swing is no easy task. It takes time, patience and practice. An exercise that Fred Couples does can be helpful to you. Fred crosses his arms, puts his hands on his shoulders and **turns at the waist from left to right** and back again all the while keeping his head facing forward. This exercise will coincide with the suggestion given by golf teachers - do the same turning motion but do it with a club in your hand and as you take the club back, turn your waist so that your buckle faces **north.** On returning, the buckle should face **south.** A good indication that you have sufficient turn is when your shoulder touches your **chin.** Some prefer their shoulder under their chin giving them more arm extension, thereby, giving them a longer arc to their swing. (shown in #2 & #3)

1.
Side view showing knee flexed inward.
The amount of knee flexing **varies** from golfer to golfer. You do need sufficient knee action to get your swing started.
Follow the arrows.

2.
BUCKLE NORTH
In case you can't turn enough for your buckle to face north, **avoid making a federal case out of it.** Many golfers, like myself, can go only so far due to physical problems. We can, however, make the buckly face south by following through with our swing as Illus. #3 shows.

3.
BUCKLE SOUTH

RIGHT   LEFT

Illustration #3

Balance & weight transfer

exercise 1

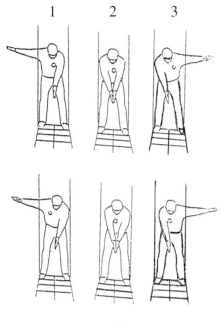

This **drill** will help you to develop balance and weight transfer

Let's use the floor tiles and follow the diagram. Standing slightly bent over, place both hands together, raise the right arm back in the same manner as you would a golf club and return the arm to the center. Then raise your left arm straight out. Make sure that your body is stable and keep the head in one position.

exercise 2

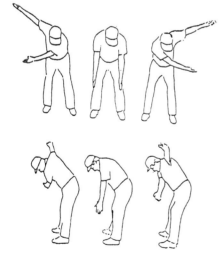

This time, hang both hands and do the swinging motion starting from right to left as though you are swinging a club. Make sure arms are swinging straight out and in. This time synchronize the arms, waist and knees in the swinging motion.

These exercises are only something to work from. If you have others by all means use them. They will be of benefit to you. Practising these exercises will develop your balance and weight transfer.

Illustration #4 **Balanced & unbalanced positions**

Models #1 & #2. The lines give an indication as to how off balance we can get by throwing our bodies **backward or forward.**

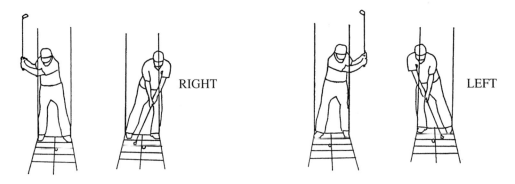

1 thru 8 show how **balanced** the body is throughout the swing.

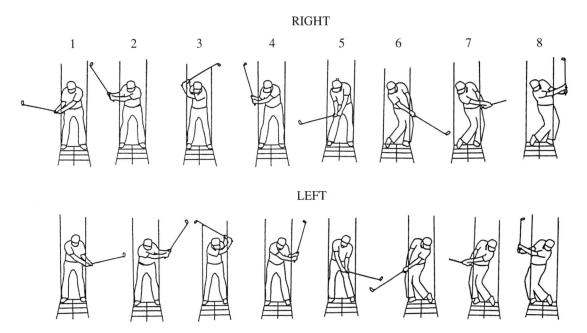

There is no question that developing a reasonable golf swing requires work. But persistence pays off. Your personal input, your stick-to-it attitude and practice will reap RESULTS!

Another common problem that beginners and misinformed golfers have is not knowing how **far** to stand from the ball at the address position. Suggestion: Stand erect and hold the club in an upright vertical position. Now, close your eyes. Next, flex the knees and take your normal posture, then, slowly lower the club to the floor with your arms in the address position. Open your eyes. That is where your ball should be placed. (This applies to all clubs).

Each club in your set will vary $1/2$" in length except from the 9-iron, the pitching wedge (PW) and the sand wedge (SW). The following chart of men's and women's club lengths are listed so that you may note and compare the differences.

Irons	Men's Modern Standard	Men's Traditional Standard	Ladies' Standard	Ladies' Petite
1	39 1/2"	39"	38"	37 1/2"
2	39"	38 1/2"	37 1/2"	37"
3	38 1/2"	38"	27"	36 1/2"
4	38"	37 1/2"	36 1/2"	36"
5	37 1/2"	37"	36"	35 1/2"
6	37"	36 1/2"	35 1/2"	34"
7	36 1/2"	36"	35"	34 1/2"
8	36"	35 1/2"	34 1/2"	34"
9	35 1/2"	35"	34"	33 1/2"
PW	35 1/2"	35"	34"	33 1/2"
SW	35 1/2"	35"	34"	33 1/2"

Woods	Men's standard	Ladies' Standard	Ladies' Petite
1	43"	42"	41 1/2"
2	42 1/2"	41 1/2"	41"
3	42"	41"	40 1/2"
4	41 1/2"	40 1/2"	40"
5	41"	40"	39 1/2"
6	40 1/2"	39 1/2"	39"
7	40"	39"	38 1/2"
8	39 1/2"	38 1/2"	38"
9	39"	38"	37 1/2"

Illustration #5 will not only help you to understand where you should position yourself in relation to other clubs but also what effect it has on your posture, balance and lie of the club.

The drawing shows 6 balls. The furthest ball from the player is placed for a driver, followed by a 3 wood, 4 wood, 2 iron, 5 iron and a 7 iron. (closest to him). #1 is in the proper 3 wood position. If he were to hit the ball in front of him, he will have to **stretch** because the ball is actually placed for a driver. This in turn will affect his **stance and lie position.** Model #2 will explain further.

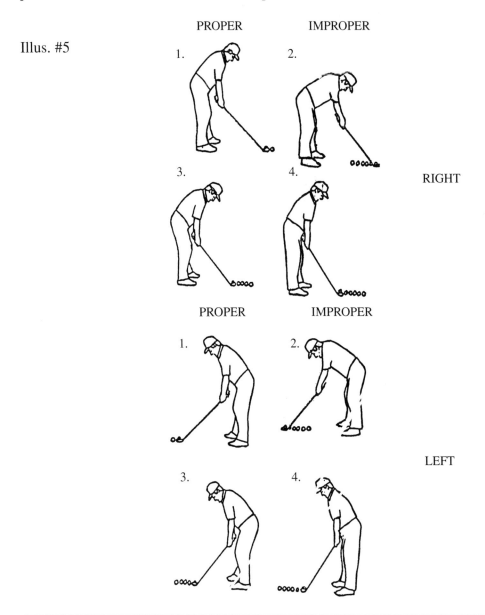

Model #2 has a 7 iron. He is **reaching out** to position himself to where the driver should be. Note the difference in posture and hand placement. Not only is he off balance, the **angle** of his club will have an adverse effect on the ball. The proper position for the club in his hand would be for the ball closest to his feet.

Model #3 is the normal set-up for a 5 iron.

Model #4 depicts the **opposite** of #2. He is using a 2 iron where normally a 7 iron would be positioned. Note how erect his is and how close his hands are to his body. Once again, the lie angle would change drastically. The heel of the club will come up.

Illus. #5

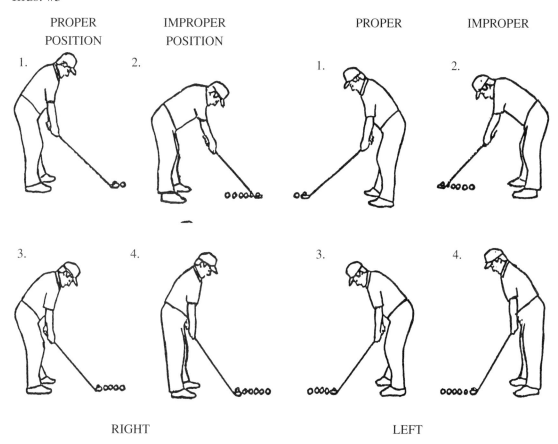

So the key to playing is either getting closer to the ball or farther away from it. **The lie angle becomes critical.** This is one reason there are so many errant shots so learn to position yourself correctly according to your chosen club. **Lunging** at the ball will only throw you off balance. Practice will help you there. Get yourself a cozy set-up and let it ride.

Illustration #6   Proper driver & 5 iron posture stance, ball and hand positions.

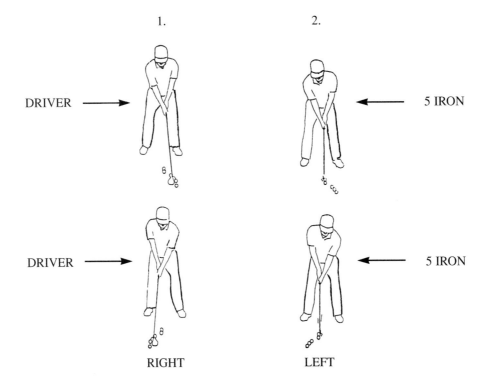

These measurements were taken using a 5'8" individual. Differing heights, length of arms and legs create oodles of variations. This illustration only goes to show what can and what does happen if we do not position ourselves correctly. Make sure that you are standing neither too close nor too far from the ball. **Trial and error** will dictate what is best for you.

Illustration #7

A proper stance and the right distance for each club will give you the maximum power from your swing. For instance, a greenside bunker stance wouldn't be appropriate to hit a driver for distance. The diagram below gives the **top view** of feet and ball placement in relation to specified clubs.

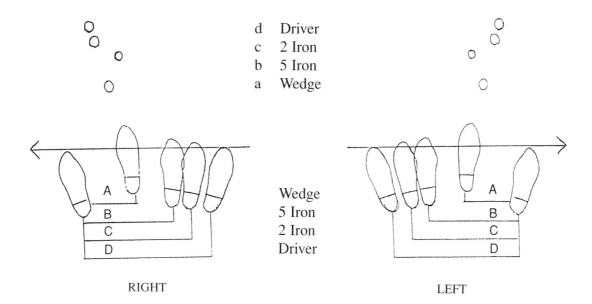

d	Driver
c	2 Iron
b	5 Iron
a	Wedge

Wedge
5 Iron
2 Iron
Driver

RIGHT   LEFT

Once your feet are planted in the proper position, toe in or toe out is a matter of preference. Some have the right foot square and the left slightly opened. (opposite for lefties)

*** Abnormal stances will be required for abnormal situations. One example would be having to hit the ball from a kneeling position. Another would be having one leg in water and the other on land.

The key to any stance, normal or abnormal, is **balance** while swinging the club.

Illustration #8

Shown are a few **normal** golf stances. Note feet positions.

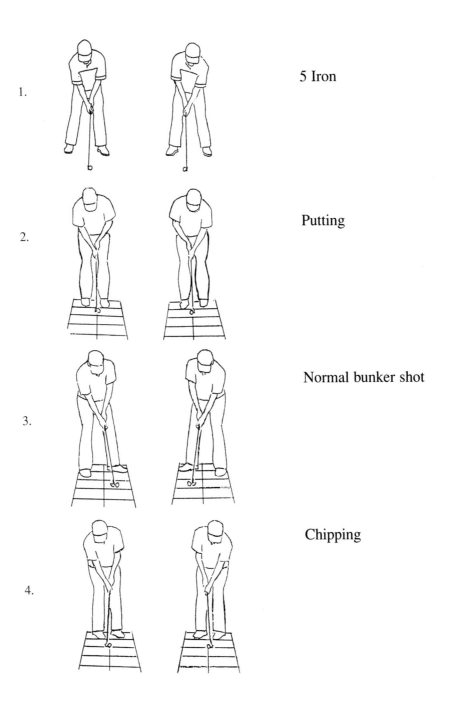

1.   5 Iron

2.   Putting

3.   Normal bunker shot

4.   Chipping

Another common problem

Illustration #9 focuses on a critical problem - the **flat** swing. The club is taken back like a tennis racket. This causes a loss of balance.

Model #1a. gives a rear view indicating the location of the club.

Model b. shows a front view. Just about anything can go wrong with this swing. This swing needs adjustment. The more moving parts, the more chances of it breaking down.

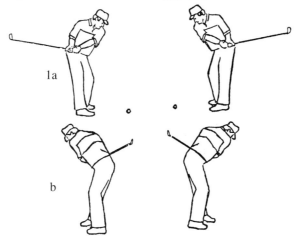

Model #2 helps us to **correct** the situation. All you need to do is practice bringing the club back **straight**, waist high, and return waist high. You can see that it eliminates the flat swing immediately.

RIGHT   LEFT

Model #3 To help you accomplish this drill, put something (chair) directly behind you and take the club back to that object, keeping it straight. **Use the lines on floor tiles as a guide.**

The drills on arm swinging in this book will also help. See page 93.

Illustration #10

Note the club positions of the **upright swing** compared to that of the **flat swing** (models 1, 2, & 3). The golfer with the flat swing is losing maximum power and accuracy.

Solution: Either practice the drill prescribed or be content to make the most of your present swing. YOU WILL SURVIVE.

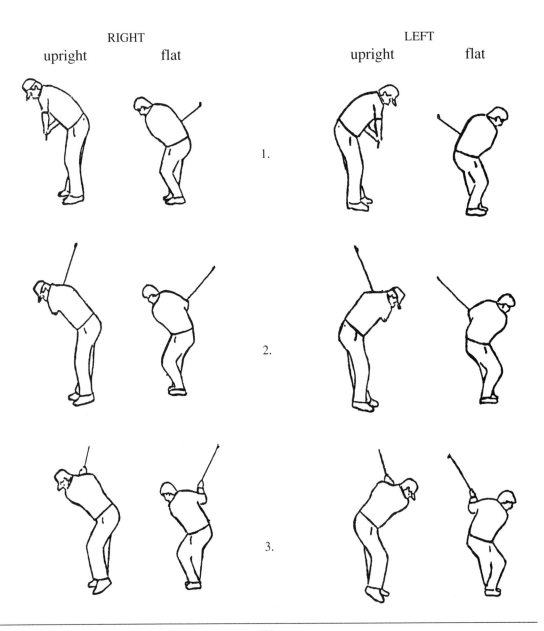

CHAPTER

CLUBFACE ANGLE AND SWINGPATH

Illustration #11

All golfers, when swinging a golf club, will either have a swing path that is inside out, square or, the most common, outside in. The drawings below show three swing path directions. Each of these swing paths will have an effect on the directional flight of the ball.

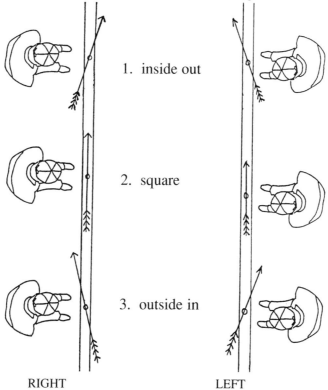

1. inside out

2. square

3. outside in

RIGHT   LEFT

The clubface angle is more crucial that the clubface path because it will influence the initial direction of the ball. The ball will be struck at **impact** by either having the **clubface open, square or closed.**

The following illustration will show three clubface angles for irons. (The clubface angle for woods is much more severe. See your clubmaker if you are having trouble with your woods).

Illustration #12   CLUBFACE ANGLE

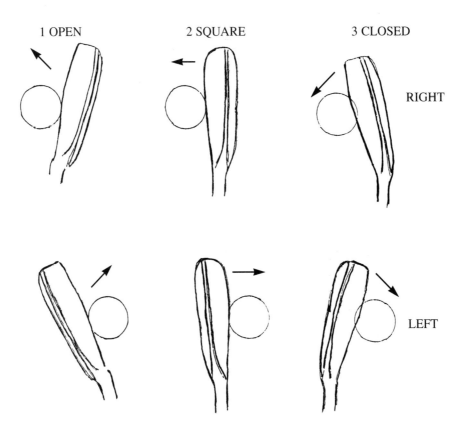

At address, keep the clubface square to the ball on take off and when you return to make impact. What you do with the club in mid air (i.e., bounce the club off your head or wrap the shaft around your neck) is not the issue. Returning the clubface angle **squarely** to the ball <u>at impact</u> is.

To help you with this, do the waist high to waist high drill.(next page) Using the 5 or 7 iron, practice this drill while keeping your arms straight as you go in each direction. Grip down on the club and stand closer to the ball with the clubface square. Make sure to keep your head at one level and stationary-not bobbing about. Good practice for knee flex as well. (See picture with drill).

Illustration #13   THE DRILL

The object of this drill is to hit the ball consistently straight. It resembles a punch shot. Bring the club back straight, waist high. Return the club forward waist high keeping your left arm straight to the target.

RIGHT   1.   LEFT

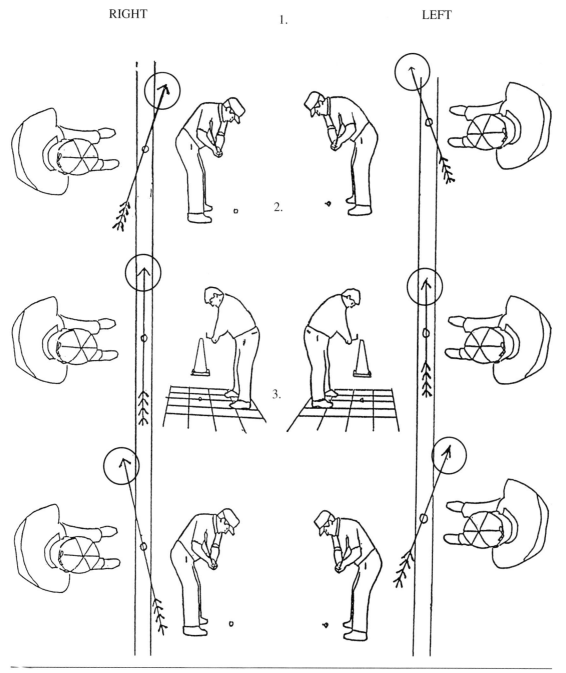

CHAPTER 31

MY RECOMMANDED DRILL

It is the desire of every golfer to play good golf. In order to achieve this, he has to keep the ball in play. That means he has to hit the fairways. The question: How do you hit the fairway? Answer: With a straight shot. Question: How do you learn to hit a straight shot?

The drill I use has proven effective and I am happy to share it with you. As an inventor, I try to make matters easier for myself, not complicated. Likewise I would like to make it easier for you. Just follow the instructions and illustrations below, and you, too, will experience straighter shots.

1a

b

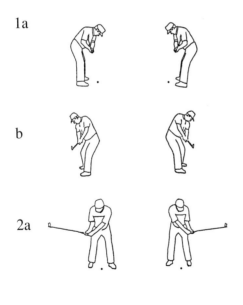

Models 1a & b show a rear view and a front view of taking the club back **waist high** and returning it **waist high.**
Make sure you keep your arms straight as you go in each direction.

2a

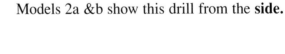

Models 2a &b show this drill from the **side.**

b

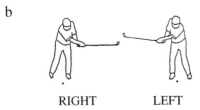

RIGHT   LEFT

Learn to hit balls to the 50 yard marker - swinging the club only waist high to waist high. Do this until you reach the 100 yard marker. There is no need to go any further. Why ruin a good thing?

Incorporate this drill into your practice session using a maximum of ten to twenty balls. Then, go about your regular practice routine. By incorporating this drill in your swing, you'll be amazed at how many straight shots you will hit in a round of golf - maybe not far, but straight. At first, you may be reluctant to try it but, in due time, you'll understand what I mean. If it works for me, why wouldn't it work for you?

CHAPTER **32**

TEMPO, TIMING AND WRIST FLEXING

Tempo is speed of movement. When your swing speed is too slow or too fast, it throws you out of sync. This, in turn, upsets your timing. Good timing is when all the body parts are in sync. Being out of sync is the reason for many mis-hits or errant shots. Body movements that are too early or too late will cause the ball to be pushed or pulled. **Timing** is as crucial to a golfer as it is to a comedian. If the timing is off, the joke bombs and nobody laughs. As they say, **timing is everything.**

A pitcher in baseball throws off-speed pitches to the batter in order to get him off stride. Likewise with our golf swing. Any jerky movement that is either too early or too late will have the same effect as an off-speed pitch. You will throw yourself **off stride, off balance,** causing a mis-hit.

There are many great golfers but few who have good timing. Moe Norman is one of those who have great timing. That is why he is the straightest ball striker in the world, even at the age of sixty-five. Moe maintains the same tempo swing after swing, never deviating from his tempo. Does that give you a hint? Does John Daly hit long straight drives every time he steps up to hit a ball? Long, yes, but not straight. We hit more balls off line than we do on line. All the body parts must be in sync in order to have good timing. Having rhythm or tempo improves that timing.

WRIST ACTION

What is wrist breaking? or is it wrist cocking or wrist flexing? To my mind, it should be flexing because we bend our wrists at a joint that is controlled by the 'flexor' muscle. It is not called the breaking muscle or the cocking muscle but the **flexor** muscle. I don't want to belabor the point but whoever heard of 'cocking your knees'? Personally, I find wrist cocking an inappropriate terminology and it is politically incorrrect.

When does the wrist flex in the upswing and when does it flex in the downswing? Is it a sudden snap? To understand this better, sit holding a hammer on your knee. Raise it up and down 6 inches. Do you feel that flexing of the wrist? Now, from the knee position, take the hammer back to your shoulder in one piece. Do this a few times. You should experience no flexing at the wrist because you are throwing back the hammer straight from your elbow. Do it again, only this time, make as though you are going to hit a nail just beyond your knee. Do it a few more times. Did you notice that as you came down from the shoulder, you flexed your wrist just as you hit the nail? If you flexed before, you would either hit the nail on the side or miss it altogether.

The hammer wrist action and the golf wrist action are very similar. As you take the club back, the wrist will gradually flex until it reaches its maximum. As the club returns, in just about that split second, the wrist will flex or at impact. My father-in-law was just such a wrist player. There was so much power in his forearms that all he needed was that flex or snap of his wrists and the ball was gone. Hank Aaron, the home run king, has the same snap or flex at impact but he also had the timing to go with it.

Your take away and **arm extension** will determine when the wrist will flex and this **varies** from golfer to golfer. One thing is certain, the wrist must flex back at impact. Too early or too late will cause a mis-hit. The arrows in the illustration show the wrist flexing gradually until it reaches its maximum.

Illus. #1

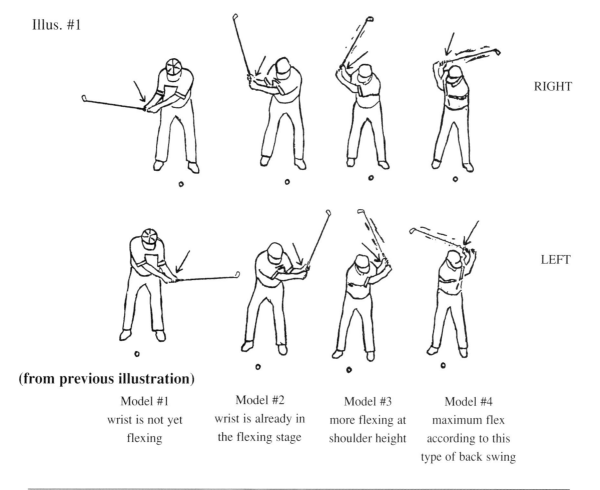

RIGHT

LEFT

(from previous illustration)

Model #1	Model #2	Model #3	Model #4
wrist is not yet flexing	wrist is already in the flexing stage	more flexing at shoulder height	maximum flex according to this type of back swing

Illustration #2   DOWNSWING FLEXING

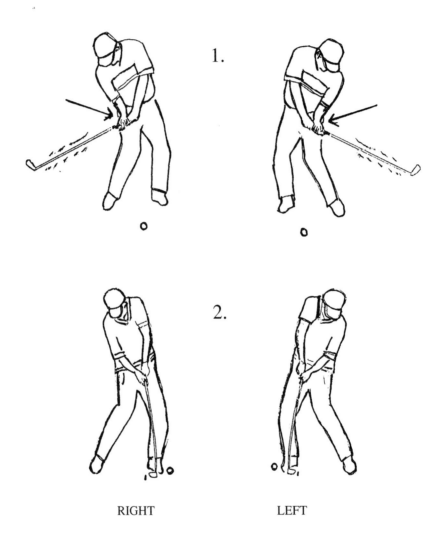

1.

2.

RIGHT   LEFT

Model #1   shows wrist is not flexed

Model #2   wrist has flexed at impact. Note the hand position, it
            is no longer flexed. The ball is airborne and the shaft
            is bowed.

CHAPTER

BE CREATIVE

"Necessity is the mother of invention"

Golf is a game that requires innovation. Why? Mis-hits, off-line or poorly executed golf shots put golfers in the most unusual, unsuspecting and precarious situations. These you-name-it situations take imagination and 'moxie' to pull off a miracle, or recovery shots as they are called.

Rather than taxing their brains, some golfers would much rather just take a stroke penalty. It's an easier and sometimes less costly way out. Aside from an unplayable lie, hitting under, over and through trees calls for creativity and steel nerves leaving you with an object lesson via the experience.

Granted, there are occasions when the ball is absolutely 'unplayable'. Rule 28 in the book, Decisions on the Rules of Golf, defines what an unplayable lie is and who makes the determination. An unplayable lie is a situation that leaves you with no option, whatsoever, but to take that penalty stroke. Your ball is wedged between branches, tucked under a large root or your ball sits in front of a high immovable rock are just a few of the 'unplayable' situations.

Golf affords us every opportunity to innovate, to experiment. Many a golfer has had his day made when he successfully executed an 'impossible shot'. If there is nothing on the line or you can afford the price, gamble. This is the part of the game that I enjoy as it gets the old adrenaline pumping. To be completely honest, I love doing it even when the stakes are high but, oh, the agony of defeat when it doesn't work out.

Never be fearful or timid in trying a shot. Golf is a game of **trial and error.** It's how we learn and by holding back, we lose out on experience. I want you to capture that feeling, knowing you tried.

So, go for it. What have you got to lose? Look at what you have to gain. Experience, confidence and moxie are the off-shoots of creativity and imagination. Take it from an inventor, enjoy, have fun.

CHAPTER **34**

AFTERTHOUGHTS

Beginners should learn to play on an executive course, a par three course or even just play nine holes. This will enable you to have fun while you learn which is the primary goal after all. A longer course would be too much at one time as it can be fatiguing, thereby, dampening your enthusiasm.

Golf is a whole package, an experience to be enjoyed - good weather, good friends, beautiful surroundings and life. So, when playing golf, chart out the course you play the same way that you map out a trip. Take note of the landscape, the ponds, the trees, houses alongside the course, anything that catches your attention to be remembered and to talk about later.

You're going to play golf. You are not going on a field trip, so there is no need to pack a huge bag with every club you own and then some. I would like to remind you of Mr. Francis Ouimet who, in 1913, won the British Open with just seven clubs in his bag. It goes to show you that bigger is not necessarily best.

I find that many golfers hit the ball as though they were afraid that it will explode or cry out in pain. Golf balls do not have feelings or emotions - so don't be afraid to really hit that ball. How many times have I seen beginners hit anywhere from six inches to two feet behind the ball. Swing at the ball. Think of getting it airborne. If the ball could speak, it would probably say "Give me your best shot".

Golfers have a problem when they don't use enough club. They select a club and usually fall short of the green. Some golfers try to impress each other, competing inwardly, to see how far they can hit with less club. That's why it is important to know the distance you get from each club. Know what your club can do and proceed accordingly.

Golf requires free movement of the body parts especially the upper part. Wearing loose clothing will help you swing the club freely with no restrictions. Tight clothing prohibits free movement.

When marking your balls for I.D., why not paint arrows on them? When putting, you can line up the arrow markings toward the hole.

Whenever you hold a club, make sure the toe of the clubface is always facing upward and not sideways. This makes the club easier to swing as it will always be in a playing position with no need to adjust at the last minute.

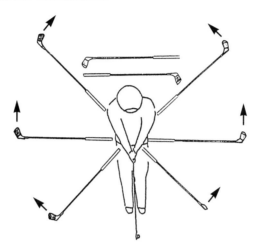

Ball position in relation to the clubface.

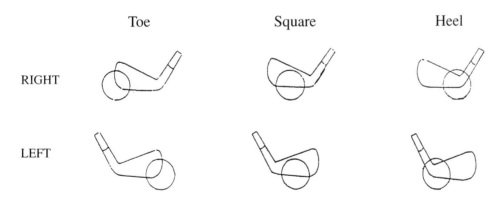

To hit the ball square, place the ball square to your clubface. If not, you will have to **compensate** somewhere in your swing in order to hit the ball squarely. Ball position is a matter of preference. **Stay with what works for you.**

Have your swing speed checked out by a clubmaker because shafts are available at different swing speeds ranging from 60-100 mph. Having the right shaft and right swing weight will help you to swing the club with ease.

Buy yourself an illustrated book on the rules of golf. This will assist you in understanding how the game should be played. Knowing the rules of golf will work to **your** advantage, not disadvantage.

Golf etiquette should be observed by all golfers at all times. Slow play makes for a long day for others. Be considerate! Repair spike marks and avoid dragging your feet on the greens. The golf green is considered **'sacred ground'.**

The information I provide is not designed to be **'all inclusive'** but enough to get you started and get you thinking. There are more important things in life than golf. Why take the game so seriously?

I welcome your comments, remarks about the ABC's of golf so feel free to write to the author. Address information is located in the front under 'about the author'.

Note: Quantity discounts are available in bulk for training purposes, gift giving or fund raising. Contact Coyote Publishers, P.O. Box 1380, Kahnawake, Quebec, J0L 1B0.

CHAPTER

SUMMARY

I want to thank you for purchasing this book and taking the time to read it. Hopefully, something will have caught your interest. If not, at least, make you aware that golf is a fun sport and was meant to be played as such.

Whatever you may read, be it in this book or another, if you have a swing that works for you, stay with it. The golf swing has many variables to be considered. Each day of golf has its own weaknesses and strengths so it's next to impossible to pinpoint with accuracy what causes a swing to be different from one day to the next.

Making the most of your swing is the prime concern. You are the ultimate decision-maker and it will be you who will be swinging that club. Make adjustments to your swing only when it is warranted. Have a firm grip and balance throughout your swing. Play within your limitations, set reasonable and realistic goals. Practice with something specific in mind and, above all, avoid taking the game too seriously and when in doubt, always refer back to the ABC's of golf. Learn to learn in fun, never let anyone make a clone out of you. Remember, **clones have no identity.**

Activate your imagination, recognize your talents and abilities then make the most of them. Above all, stay with what works for you.

Patience, determination, a positive outlook and a stick-to-it attitude will take you down the road to success. Believe in yourself. If you're doing your best, you'll never have time to think of failure.

NO FAILURE IS EVER FINAL... NOR IS SUCCESS!

Golf, like a juggler on a unicycle, requires balance, co-ordination and practice.

Which do you think is easier to learn?

The ABC's of GOLF

GIFT ORDER FORM

Please send _____ copies of The ABC's of Golf at $24.95 U.S. funds each or $29.95 Cdn. each plus $4.95 shipping and handling per book.

Send gift to: _____

NAME: _____

ADDRESS: _____

PROV./CITY/STATE/ZIP: _____

Enclosed is my postal money order made out to COYOTE PUBLISHERS for $_____

to: COYOTE PUBLISHERS, P.O. Box 1380, Kahnawake, Quebec J01 1B0

The ABC's of GOLF

GIFT ORDER FORM

Please send _____ copies of The ABC's of Golf at $24.95 U.S. funds each or $29.95 Cdn. each plus $4.95 shipping and handling per book.

Send gift to: _____

NAME: _____

ADDRESS: _____

PROV./CITY/STATE/ZIP: _____

Enclosed is my postal money order made out to COYOTE PUBLISHERS for $_____

to: COYOTE PUBLISHERS, P.O. Box 1380, Kahnawake, Quebec J01 1B0

The
ABC's
of
GOLF

COMMENT CARD

Dear Reader:

We are interested in using comments from satisfied readers to tell others about this exciting new book. May we share your views as excerpted below with others? ... Or feel free to write anything additional!

_____

_____

_____

_____

_____

_____

_____

_____

_____

_____

_____

Yes, I agree that my comments may be used for national publicity and advertising. I understand that I will not receive any payment or compensation for this permission. My name or initials (circle your preference), as well as the city and state which I reside, and my occupation may also be used.

SIGNATURE: _____

DATE: _____ OCCUPATION: _____

NAME: _____

ADDRESS: _____

CITY/STATE/ZIP: _____

PROV./POSTAL CODE: _____

THANK YOU.